SPATIAL REASONING TESTS

www.How2Become.com

To help you further understand Spatial Reasoning Test Questions watch our FREE video at the following page:

www.SpatialTests.co.uk

Get more products for passing any test or interview at:

www.How2Become.com

Orders: Please contact How2Become Ltd, Suite 1, 60 Churchill Square Business Centre, Kings Hill, Kent ME19 4YU. You can also order via the e mail address info@how2become.com.

ISBN: 978-1909229723

First published in 2014 by How2Become Ltd

Updated in 2018.

Typeset for How2Become Ltd by Anton Pshinka.

CONTENTS

As part of this product you have also received FREE access to online tests that will help you to pass Spatial Reasoning Tests

To gain access, simply go to:

www.PsychometricTestsOnline.co.uk

INTRODUCTION TO YOUR NEW GUIDE

Dear Sir/Madam,

Welcome to your new guide, *Spatial Reasoning Tests*. This guide contains lots of sample test questions that are appropriate for anyone who is required to take a technical spatial reasoning test. The key to success in any career or job-related assessment is to try your hardest to get 100%. If you aim for 100% in your preparation, then you are far more likely to achieve the trade or career that you want. We have deliberately supplied you with lots of sample questions to assist you. It is crucial that when you get a question wrong, you take the time to find out why you got it wrong. Understanding the question is very important.

Finally, if you want to try out more tests that will prepare you for your assessment then we offer a wide range of products to assist you at www. How2Become.com. We have also created a FREE training video that will explain further how to tackle spatial reasoning tests at the following webpage:

www.SpatialTests.co.uk

Good luck and best wishes,

The how2become team

The How2Become team

PREFACE BY AUTHOR RICHARD MCMUNN

It's probably important that I start off by explaining a little bit about myself, my background, and also why I'm suitably qualified to help you prepare for your spatial reasoning test.

At the time of writing I am 41 years old and live in Tunbridge Wells, Kent. I left school at the usual age of 16 and joined the Royal Navy, serving on-board HMS Invincible as part of 800 Naval Air Squadron which formed part of the Fleet Air Arm. There I was, at the age of 16, travelling the world and working as an engineer on Sea Harrier jets! It was fantastic and I loved every minute of it. After four years I left the Royal Navy and joined Kent Fire and Rescue Service as a firefighter.

Over the next 17 years I worked my way up through the ranks to the position of Assistant Divisional Officer. During my time in the Fire Service I spent a lot of time working as an instructor at the Fire Brigade Training Centre. I was also involved in the selection process for assessing candidates who wanted to become firefighters. Therefore, my knowledge and experience gained so far in life has been invaluable in helping people like you to pass any type of selection process. I am sure you will find this guide an invaluable resource during your preparation for your assessment.

I have always been fortunate in the fact that I persevere at everything I do. I've understood that if I keep working hard in life then I will always be successful; or I will achieve whatever it is that I want to achieve. This is an important lesson that I want you to take on-board straight away. If you work hard and persevere, then success will come your way. It is also very important that you believe in your own abilities. It does not matter if you have no qualifications. It does not matter if you are currently weak in the area of spatial reasoning or psychometric testing. What does matter is self-belief, self-discipline and a genuine desire to improve and become successful.

Finally, as part of this product I want to give you FREE access to online tests that will help you to pass spatial reasoning tests. To gain access, simply go to:

www.PsychometricTestsOnline.co.uk

Best wishes,

Richard McMunn

Richard McMunn

DISCLAIMER

TIPS FOR PASSING SPATIAL REASONING TESTS

There's no two ways about it, the most effective way in which you can prepare for your test is to carry out lots of sample test questions. When we say lots, we mean lots! Before we provide you with a host of test questions for you to try, here are a few important tips for you to consider:

- The definition of spatial reasoning is 'The ability to interpret and make drawings from mental images and visualise movement or change in those images.' The sample test questions within this guide will help you to improve in the areas of visualising and interpreting movement in shapes and diagrams. Make sure you watch the video at www.SpatialTests.co.uk as the information there will help you understand the test questions and how best to tackle them.

- It is important that, before you sit your test, you find out the type(s) of questions you will be required to answer. You should also take steps to find out if the tests will be timed and also whether or not they will be 'multiple-choice' based questions. If the tests that you will be required to undertake are timed and of multiple-choice in nature, then we strongly advise that you practise this type of test question.

- Variety is the key to success. We recommend that you attempt a variety of different test questions, such as psychometric tests, numerical reasoning, verbal reasoning, fault analysis and mechanical reasoning etc. This will undoubtedly improve your overall ability to pass the test that you are required to undertake. You will be able to try all of these free of charge, if you go to the free tests at www.PsychometricTestsOnline.co.uk.

- Confidence is an important part of test preparation. Have you ever sat a timed test and your mind goes blank? This is because your mind is focused on negative thoughts and your belief that you will fail the test. If you practice plenty of test questions under timed conditions then your confidence will grow. If your confidence is at its peak at the commencement of the test then there is no doubt that you will actually look forward to sitting the test, as opposed to being fearful of the outcome.

- Whilst this is a very basic tip that may appear obvious, many people neglect to follow it. Make sure that you get a good night's sleep the night before your test or assessment. Research has shown that those people who have regular 'good' sleep are far more likely to concentrate better during psychometric tests.

- Aim for SPEED as well as ACCURACY. Many test centres want to see how quickly you can work, but they also want to see how accurate your work is, too. Therefore, when tackling the tests you must work as quickly as you can without sacrificing accuracy. Most tests are designed so that you do not finish them and you will most probably lose marks for incorrect answers.

- You are what you eat! In the week prior to the test eat and drink healthily. Avoid cigarettes, alcohol and food with high fat content. The reason for this is that all of these will make you feel sluggish and you will not perform at your peak. On the morning of your assessment eat a healthy breakfast such as porridge and a banana.

- Drink plenty of water, always!

- If you have any special needs that need to be catered for ensure you inform the assessment centre staff prior to the assessment day. I have met people in the past who are fearful of telling the assessment staff that they are dyslexic. You will not be treated negatively; in fact the exact opposite. They will give you extra time in the tests which can only work in your favour.

Now that we have provided you with a number of important tips, take the time to work through the many different sample test questions that are contained within the guide. You will need a stop watch in order to assess your performance against the time constraints for each test.

SPATIAL REASONING TESTS

TESTS

SECTION 1

SPATIAL REASONING TESTS SECTION 1

Take a look at the following 3 shapes. Note the letters on the side of each shape:

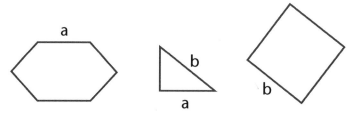

Join all of the 3 shapes together with the corresponding letters to make the following shape:

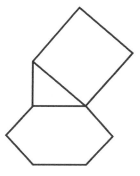

During the following spatial reasoning exercise your task is to look at the given shapes and decide which of the examples match the shape when joined together by the corresponding letters. You have 45 minutes to answer the 40 questions.

SPATIAL REASONING TEST EXERCISE 1

Question 1

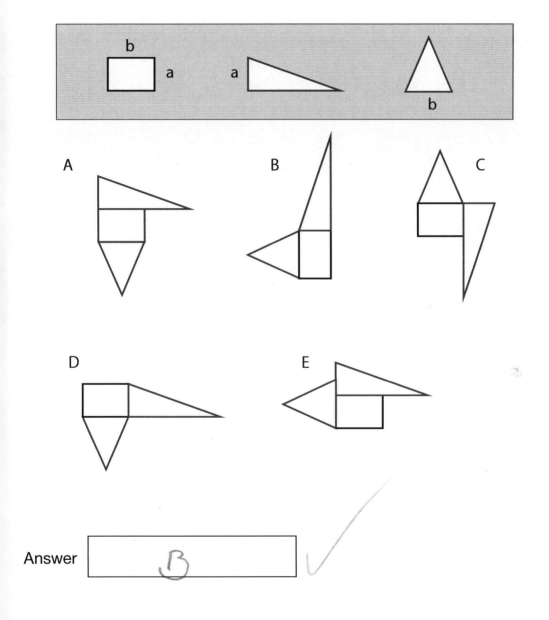

Answer [B]

Question 2

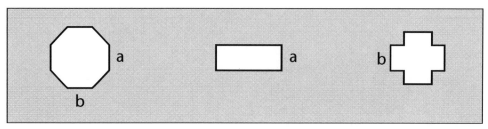

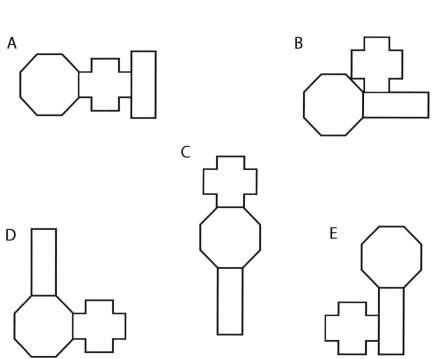

Answer [D]

Question 3

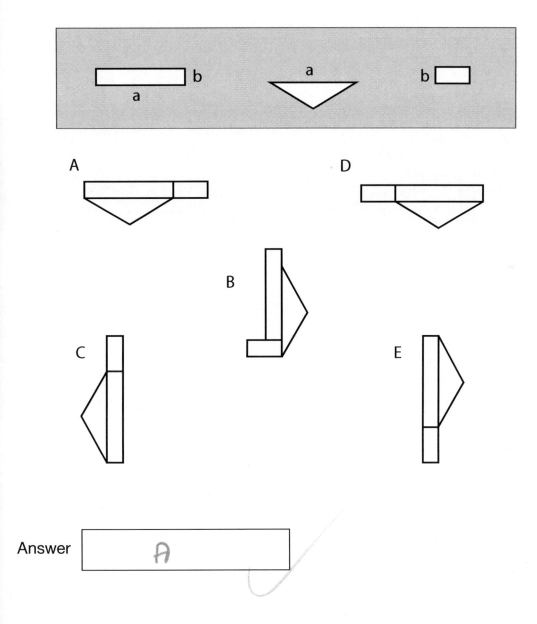

Answer | A

Question 4

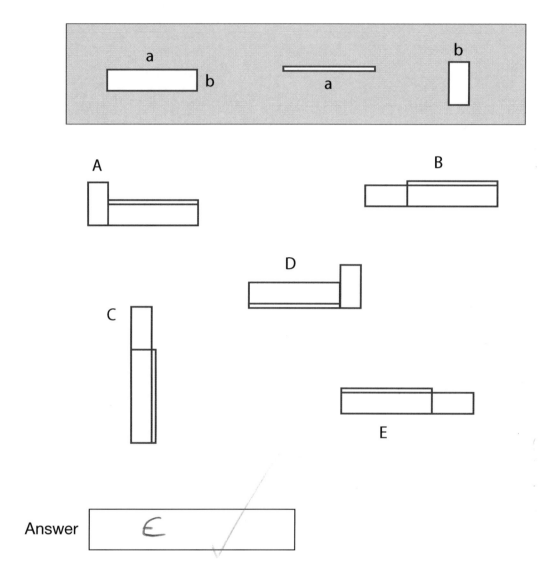

Answer   E

Question 5

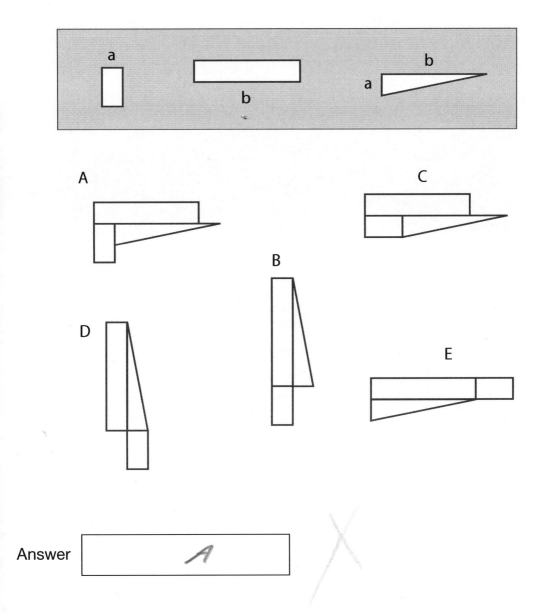

Answer [*A*]

Question 6

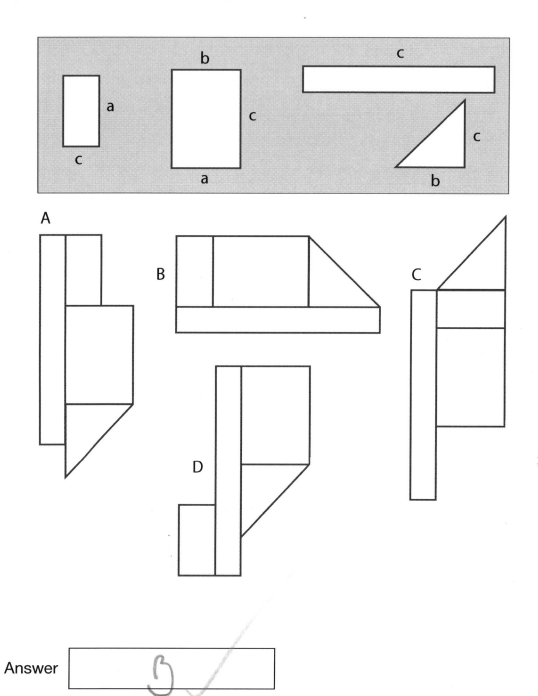

Answer

Question 7

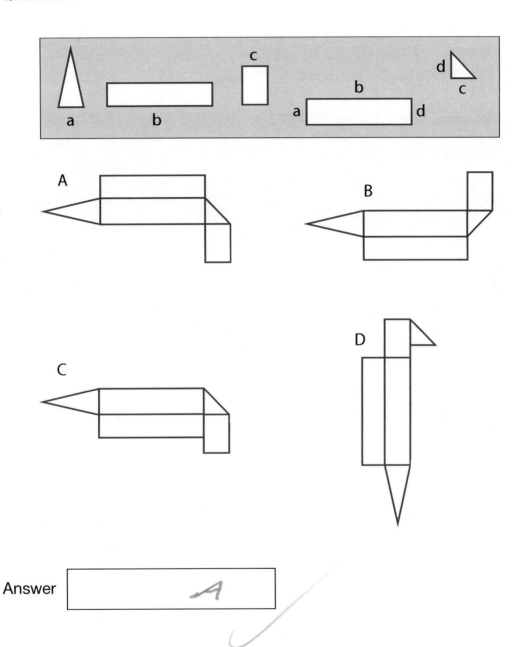

Answer

Question 8

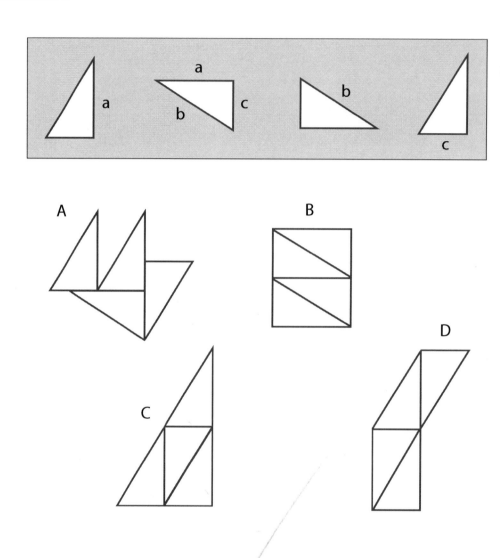

Answer C

Question 9

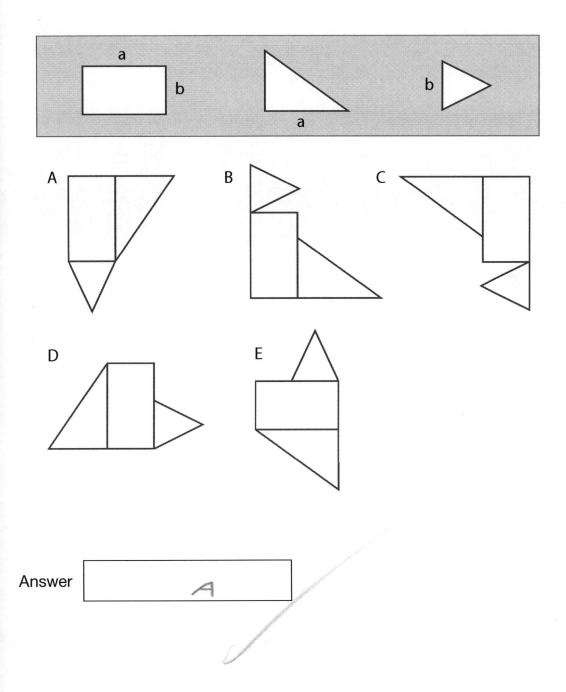

Answer [A]

Question 10

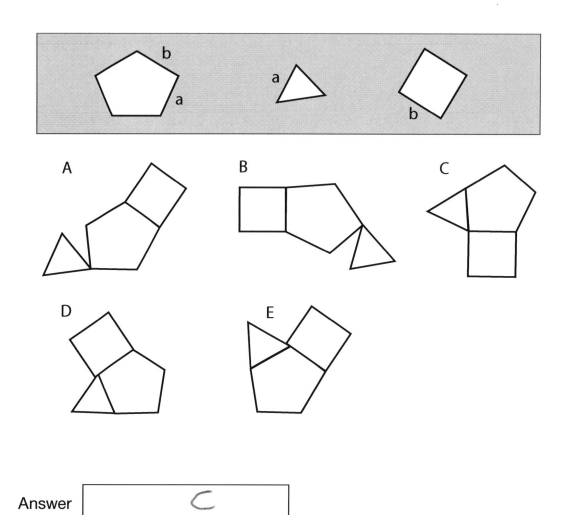

Answer | C

Question 11

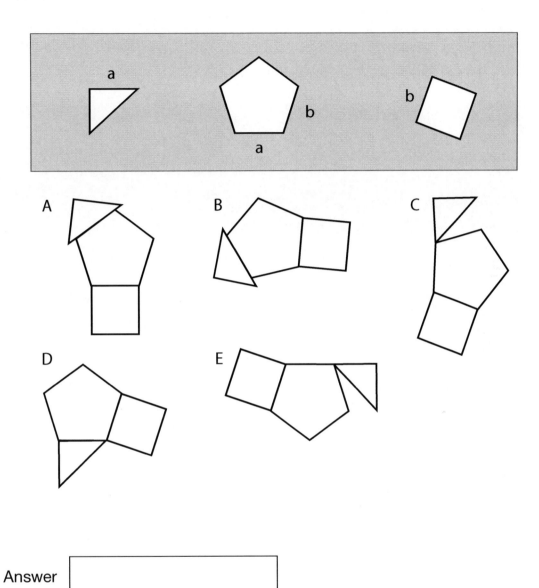

Answer

Question 12

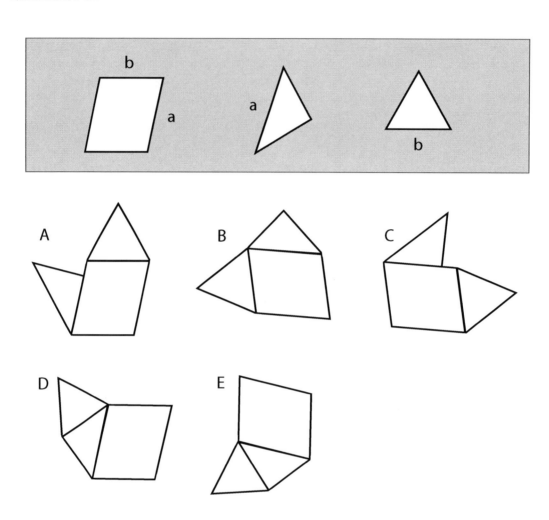

Answer

Question 13

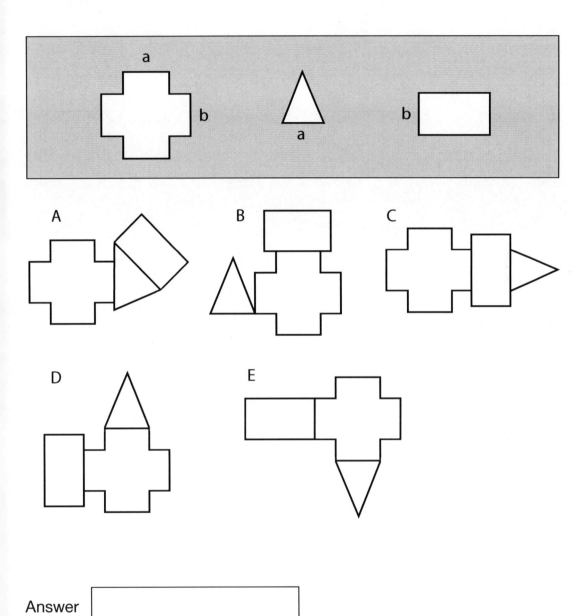

Answer _____

Question 14

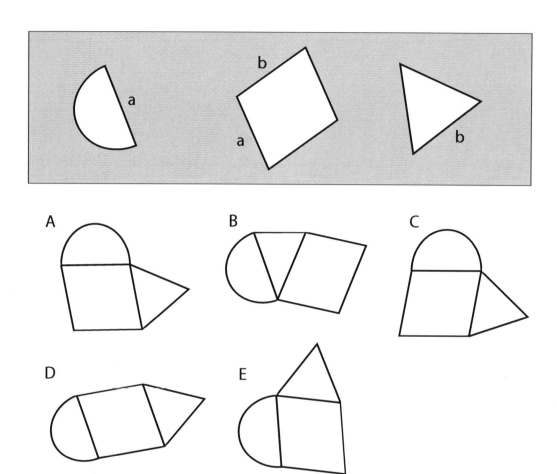

Answer

Question 15

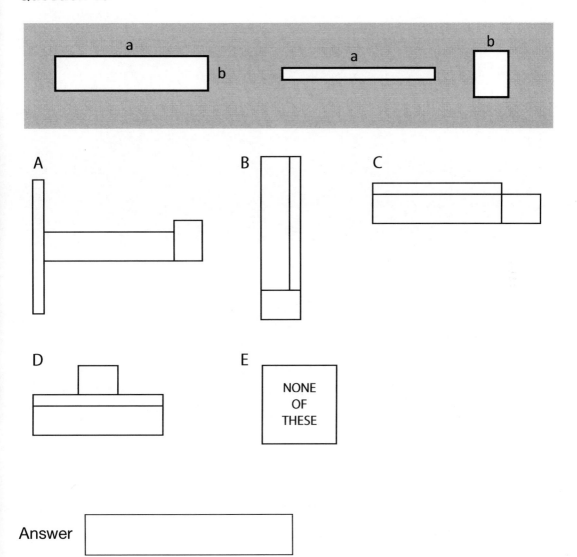

Answer

Question 16

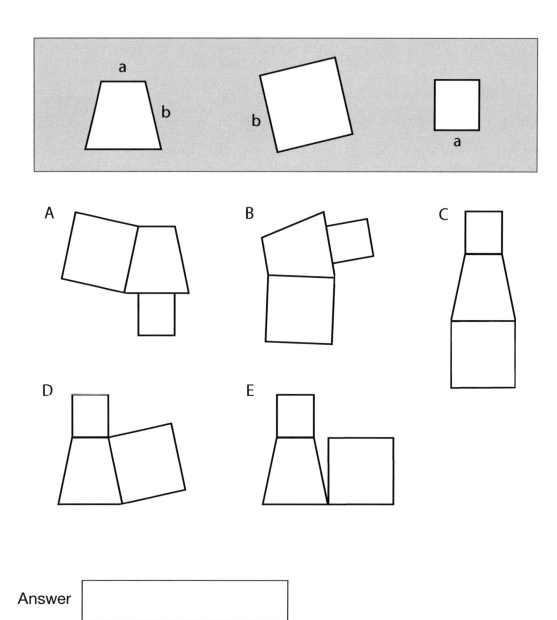

Answer

Question 17

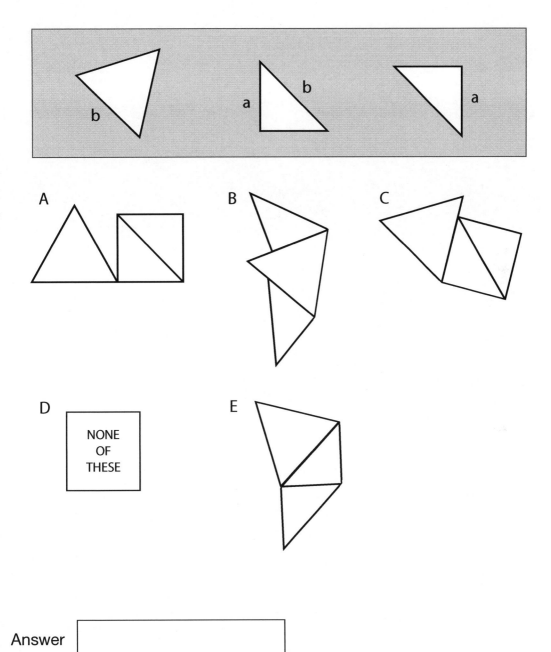

Answer

Question 18

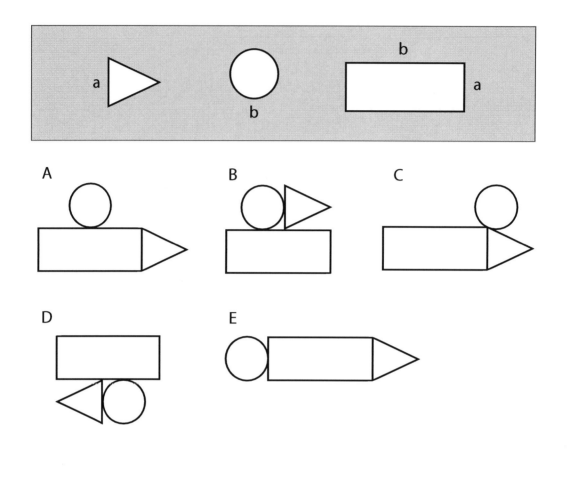

Answer

Question 19

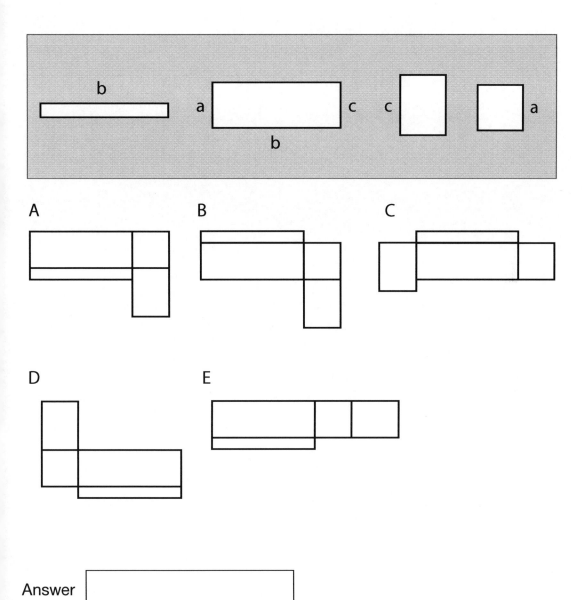

A

B

C

D

E

Answer

Question 20

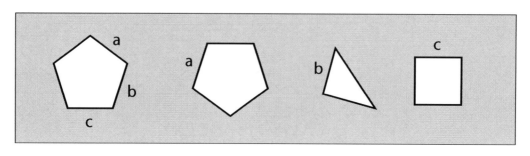

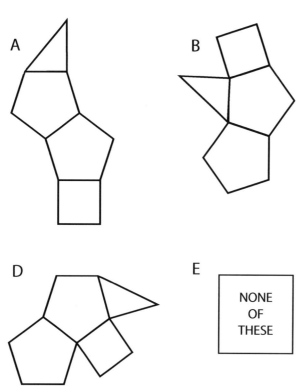

A

B

C

D

E

| NONE |
| OF |
| THESE |

Answer

Question 21

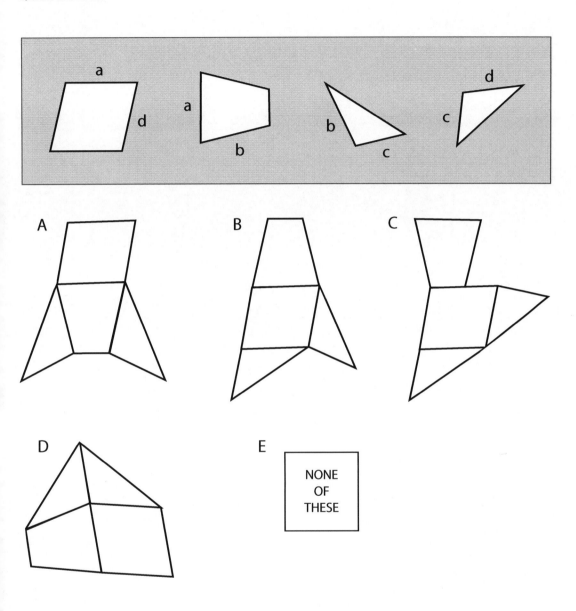

Answer

Question 22

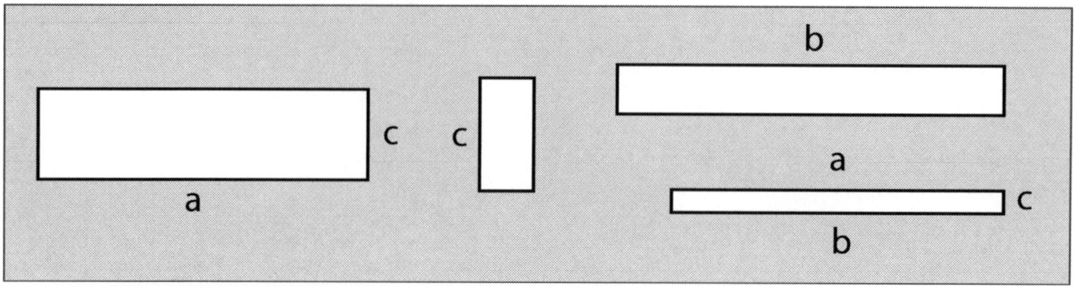

A

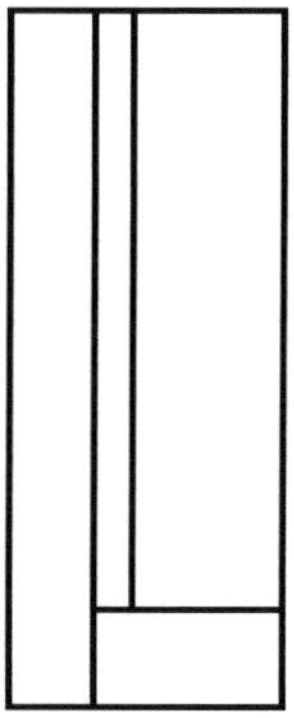

B

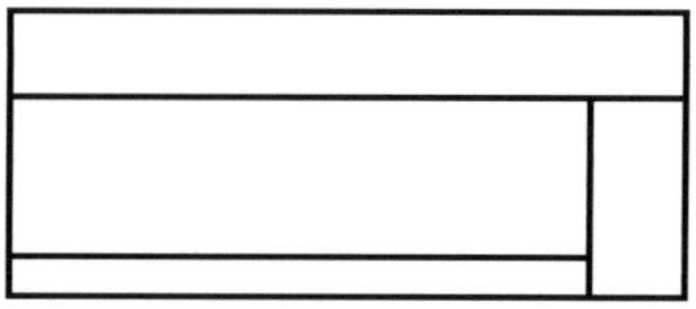

C

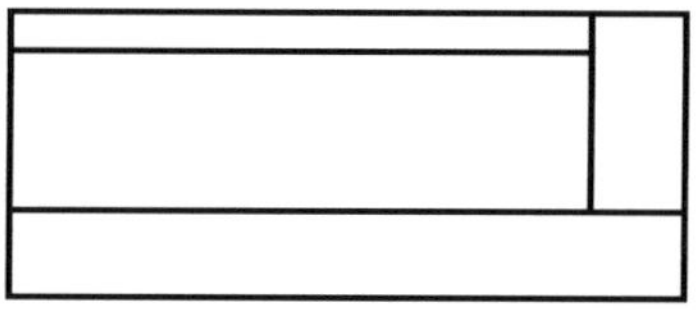

D

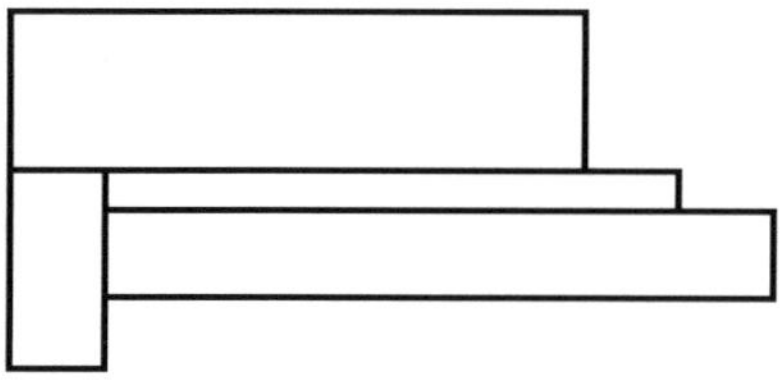

E

NONE
OF
THESE

Answer

Question 23

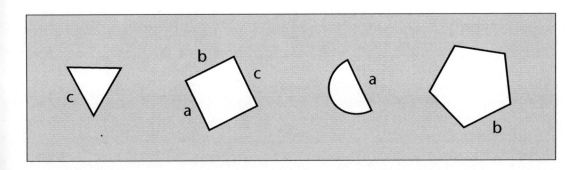

A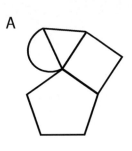

B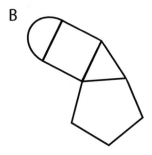

C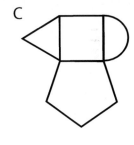

D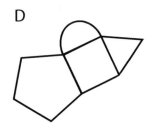

E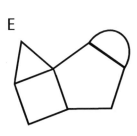

Answer

Question 24

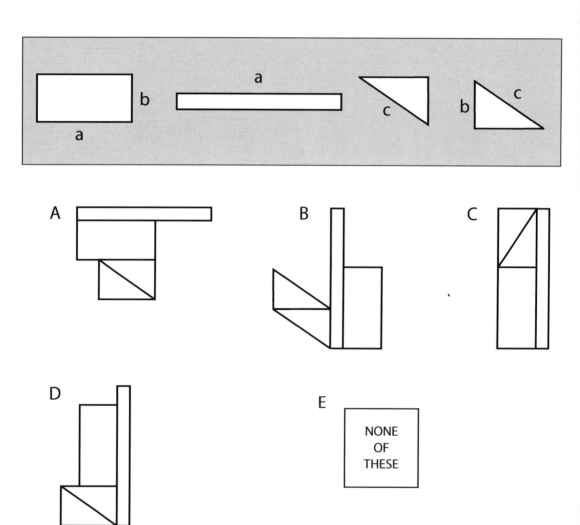

Answer

Question 25

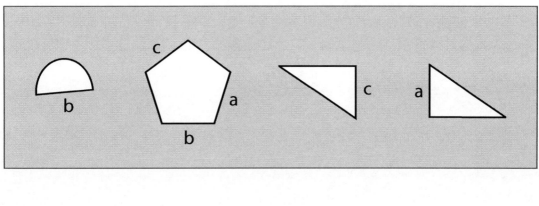

A

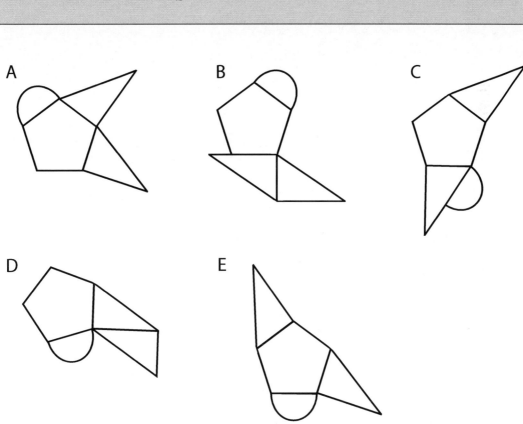

B

C

D

E

Answer

Question 26

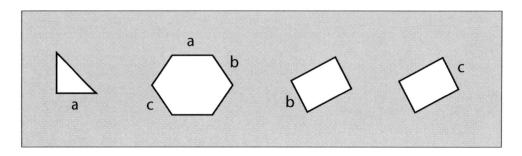

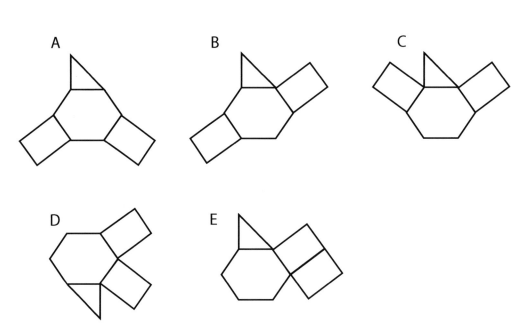

Answer

Question 27

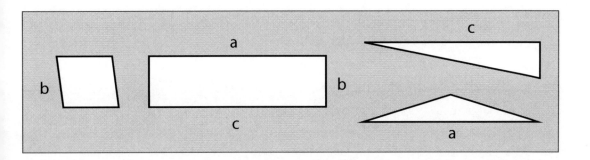

A

B

C

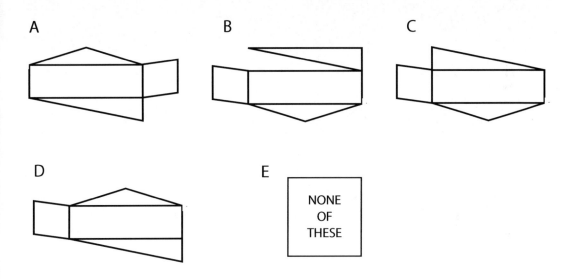

D

E

NONE
OF
THESE

Answer

Question 28

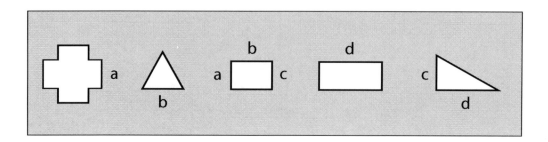

A

B

C

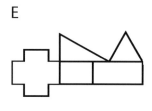

D

E

Answer

Question 29

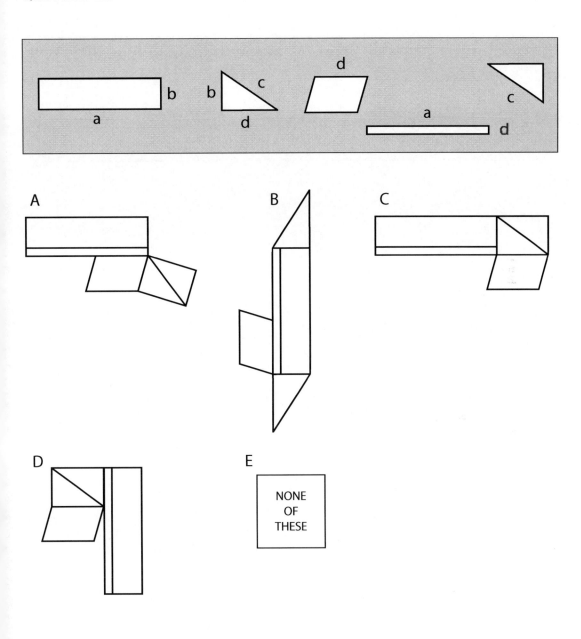

Answer

Question 30

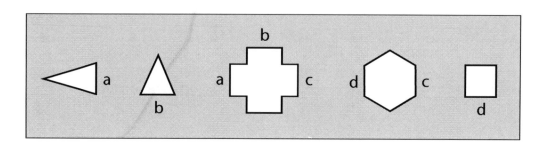

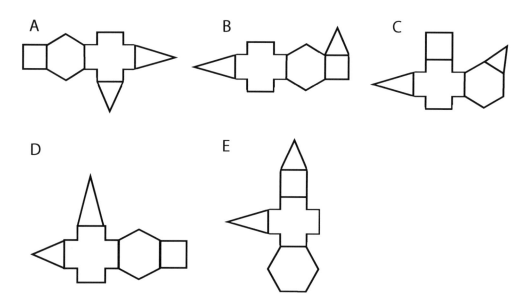

Answer

Question 31

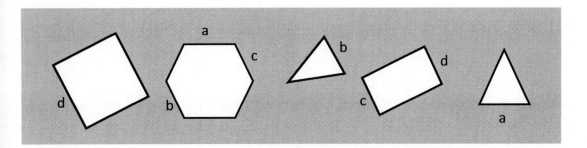

A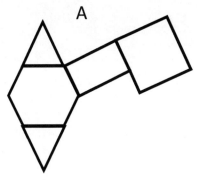

B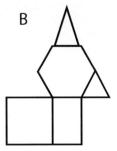

C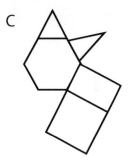

D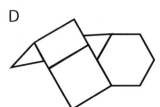

E

| NONE |
| OF |
| THESE |

Answer

Question 32

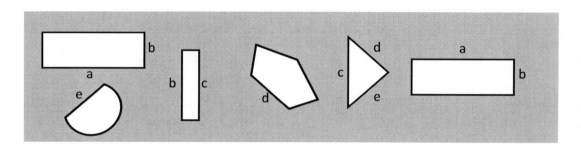

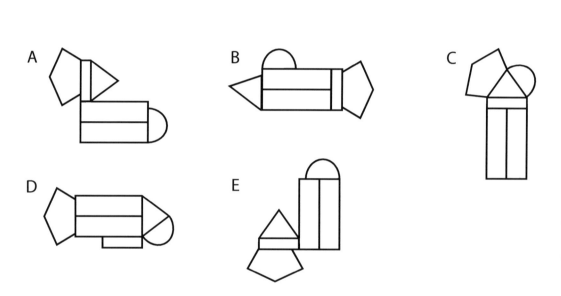

Answer

Question 33

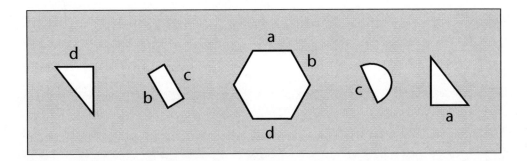

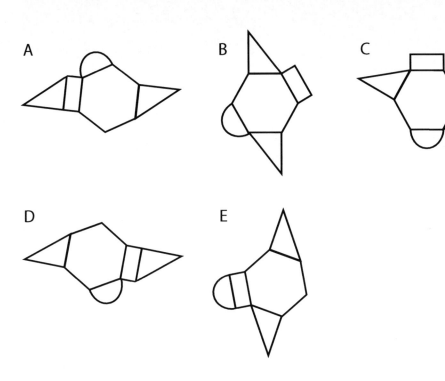

Answer

Question 34

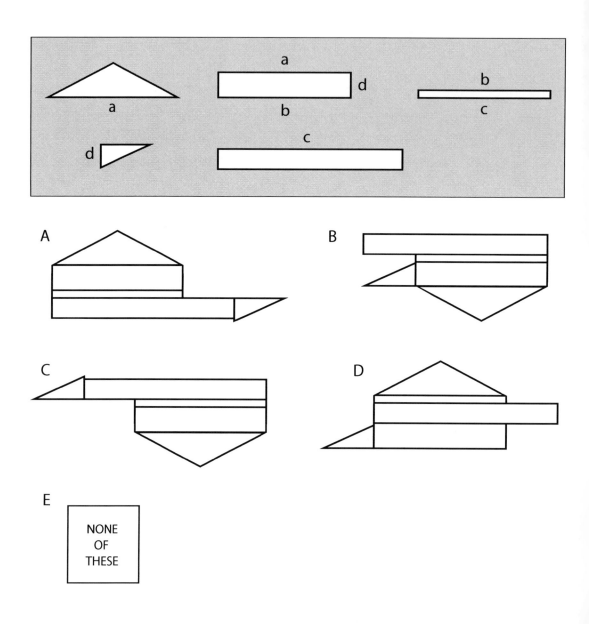

Answer [   ]

Question 35

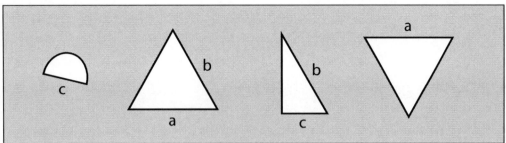

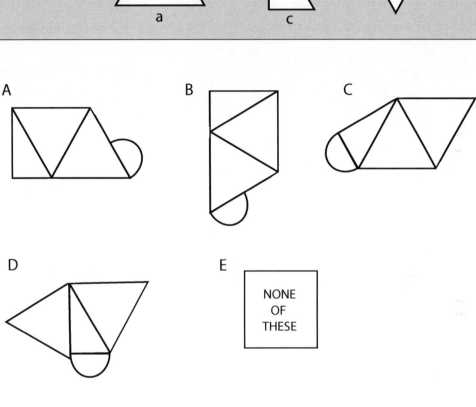

Answer

Question 36

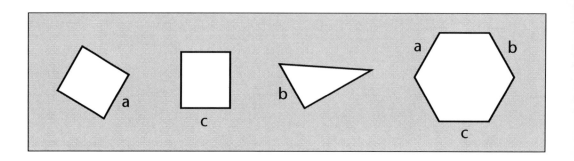

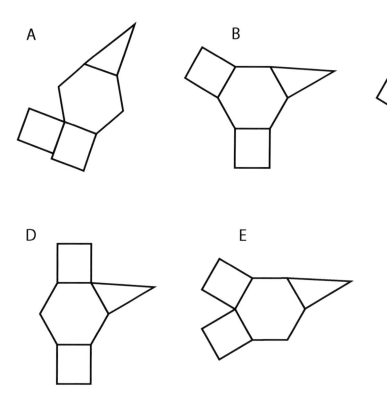

Answer [   ]

Question 37

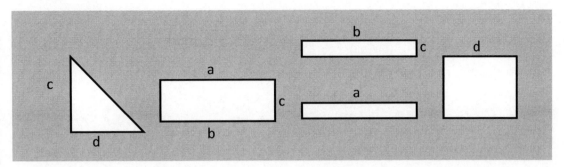

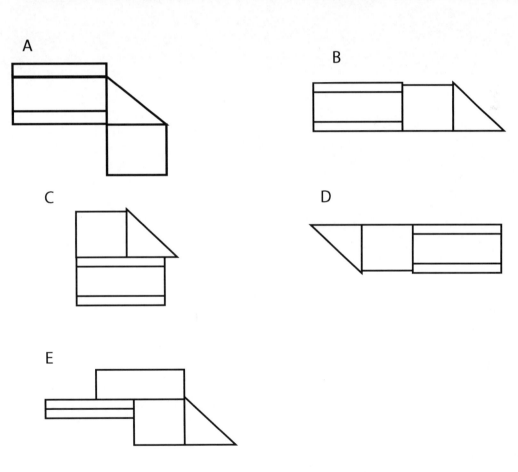

Answer

Question 38

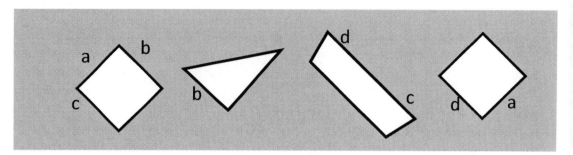

A

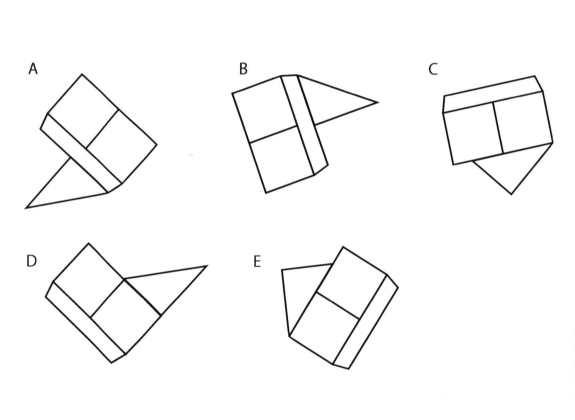

B

C

D

E

Answer

Question 39

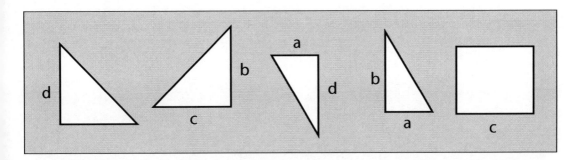

A

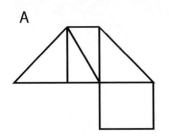

B

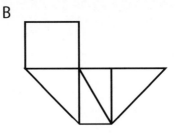

C

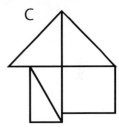

D

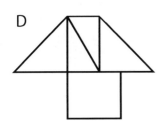

E

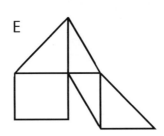

Answer

Question 40

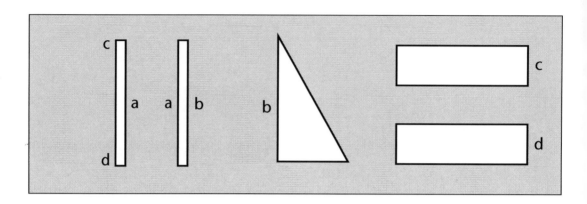

A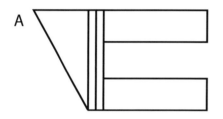

B

C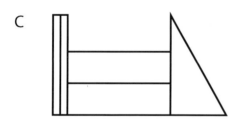

D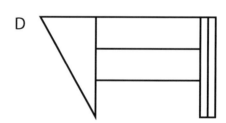

E
NONE
OF
THESE

Answer

ANSWERS TO SPATIAL REASONING TEST EXERCISE 1

Q1. B

Q2. D

Q3. A

Q4. E

Q5. D

Q6. B

Q7. A

Q8. C

Q9. A

Q10. C

Q11. D

Q12. B

Q13. E

Q14. A

Q15. C

Q16. D

Q17. E

Q18. A

Q19. C

Q20. B

Q21. E

Q22. E

Q23. C

Q24. C

Q25. E

Q26. B

Q27. E

Q28. D

Q29. E

Q30. A

Q31. E

Q32. C

Q33. E

Q34. B

Q35. C

Q36. B

Q37. A

Q38. D

Q39. E

Q40. A

Once you are satisfied with your answers, please move onto the next section of the guide.

SPATIAL REASONING TESTS

SECTION 2

SPATIAL REASONING TESTS SECTION 2

During the second spatial reasoning test that I've provided you with, you will be required to look at 3-dimensional objects. You have to imagine the 3-dimensional objects rotated in a specific way and then match them up against a choice of examples.

Both objects rotate the same amount.

Look at the 2 objects below:

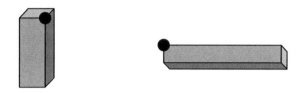

You now have to decide which of the 4 options provided demonstrates both objects rotated with the dot in the correct position. Look at the options below:

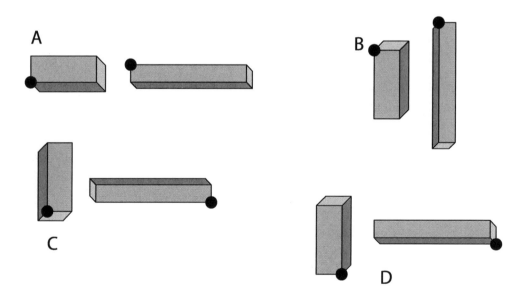

The correct answer is C

Now move on to spatial reasoning test exercise 2 on the following page. You have 45 minutes in which to complete the 40 questions.

SPATIAL REASONING TEST EXERCISE 2

Question 1

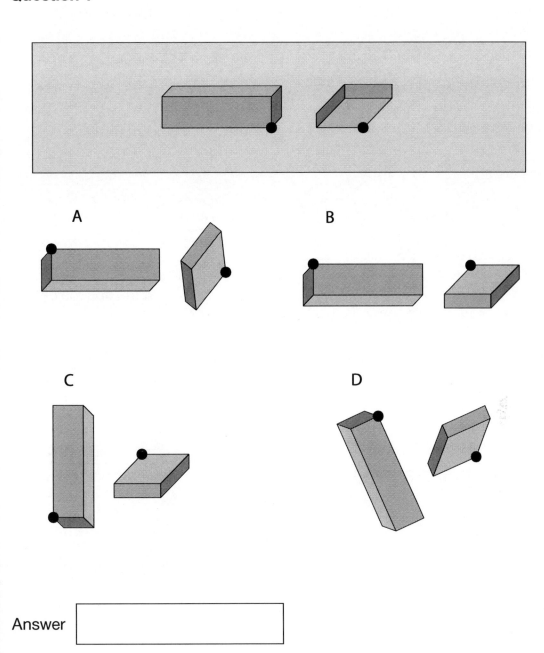

A

B

C

D

Answer

Question 2

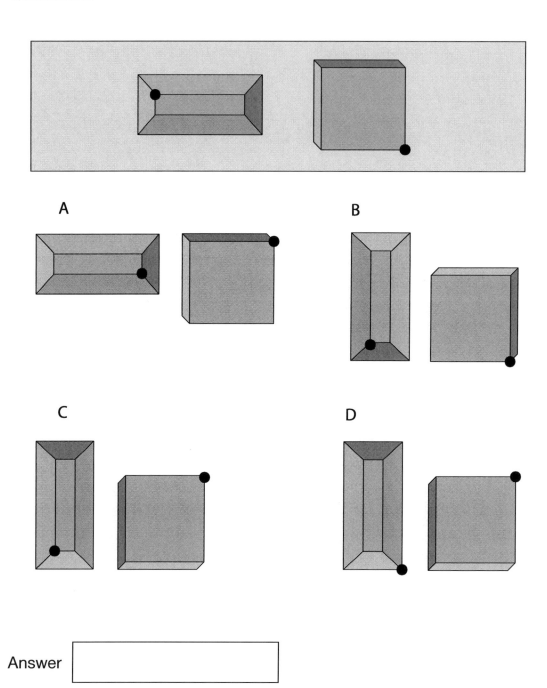

Answer

Question 3

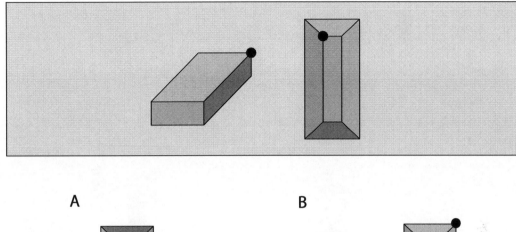

A

B

C

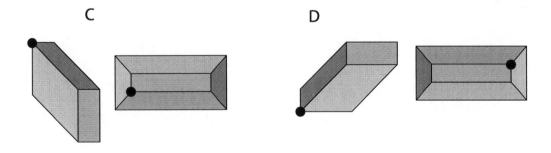

D

Answer

Question 4

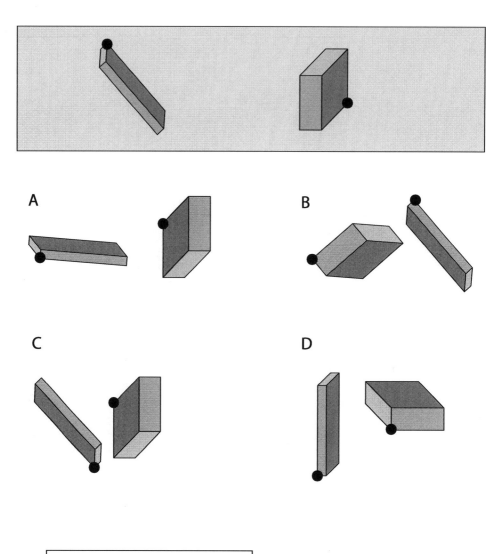

Answer

Question 5

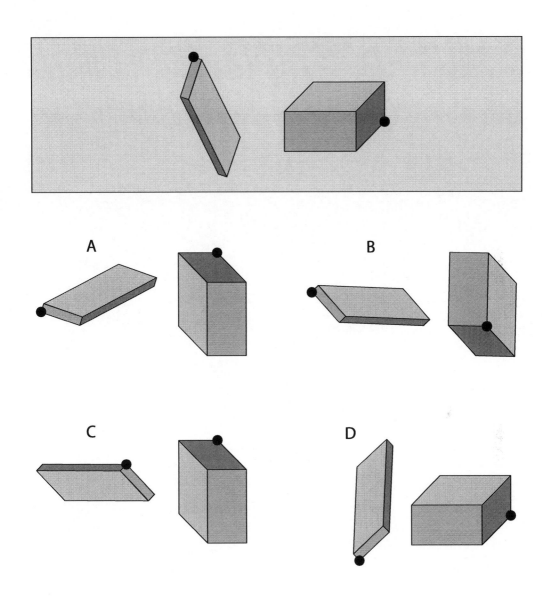

Answer

Question 6

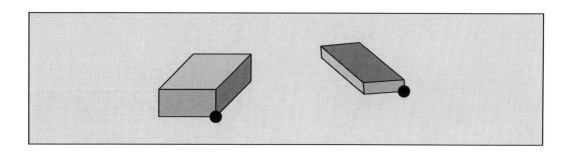

A

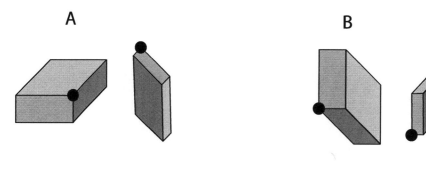

B

C

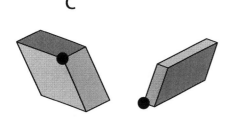

D

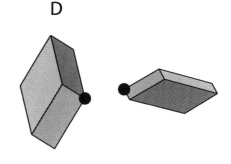

Answer

Question 7

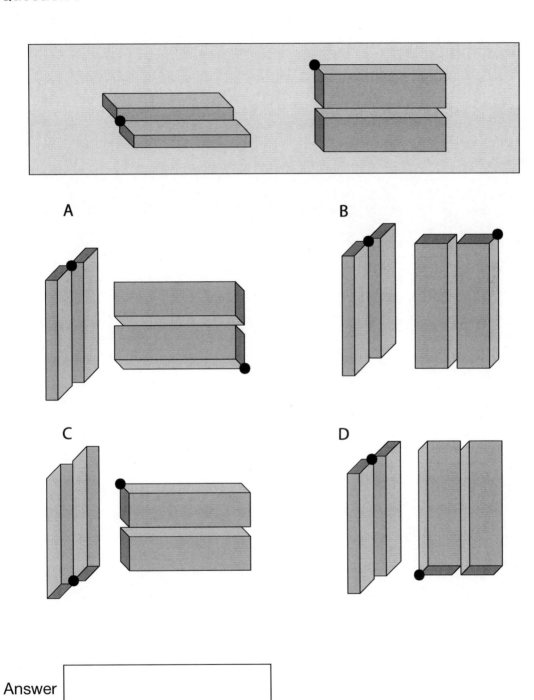

A

B

C

D

Answer

Question 8

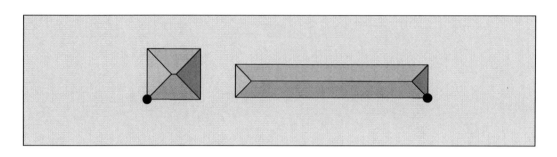

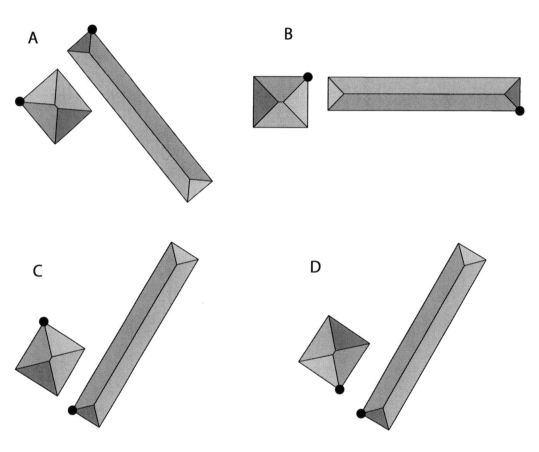

A

B

C

D

Answer

Question 9

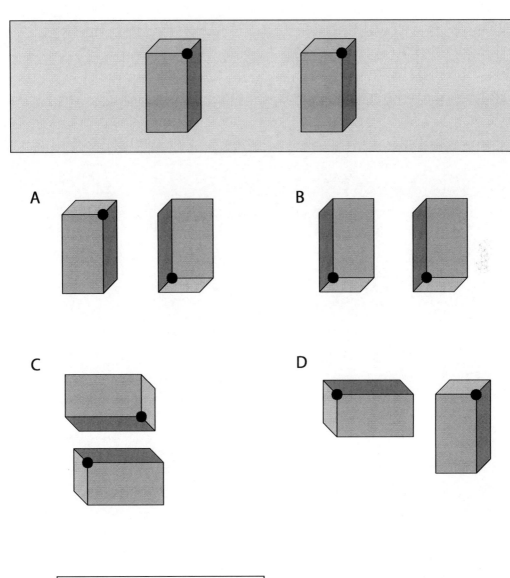

A

B

C

D

Answer

Question 10

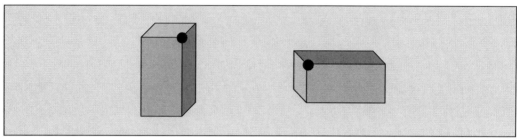

A

B

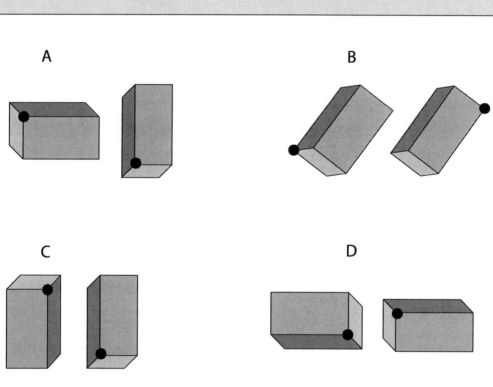

C

D

Answer

Question 11

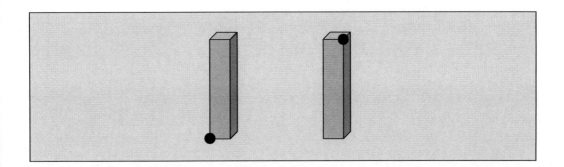

A

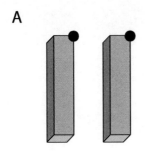

B

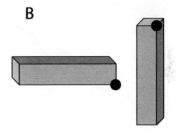

C

NONE
OF
THESE

D

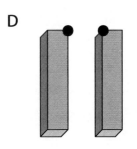

Answer

Question 12

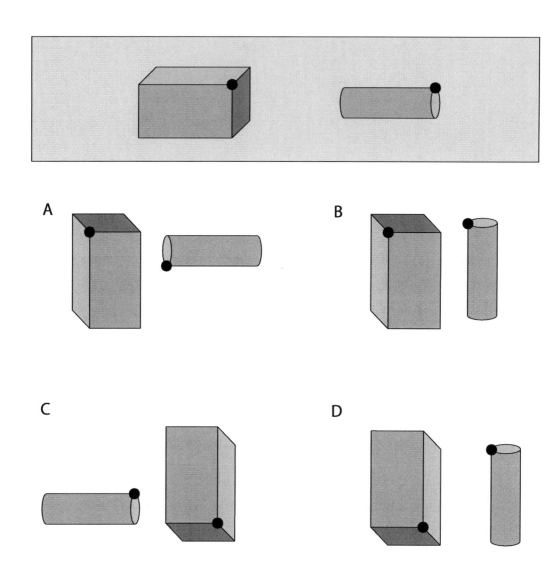

A

B

C

D

Answer

Question 13

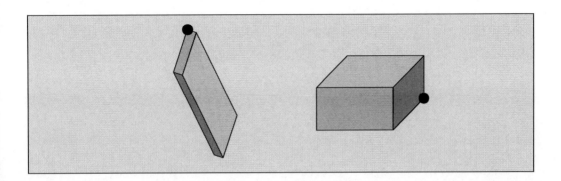

A

B

C

D

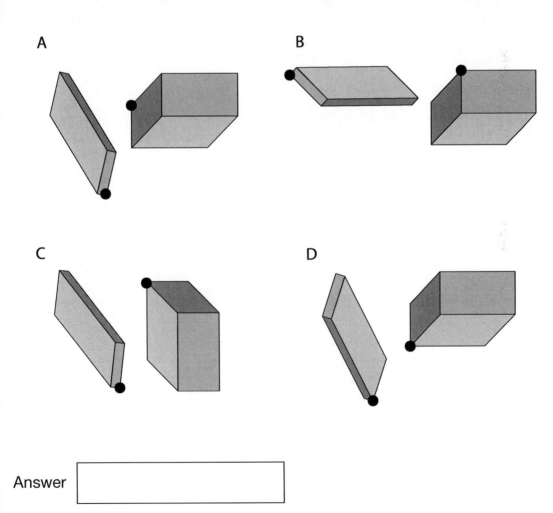

Answer

Question 14

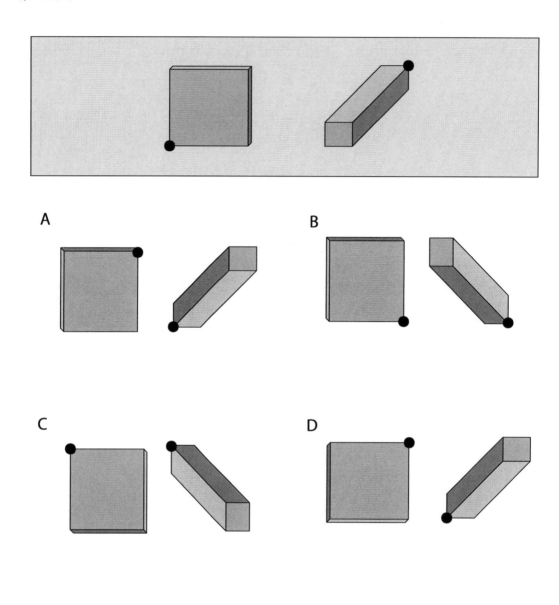

A

B

C

D

Answer

Question 15

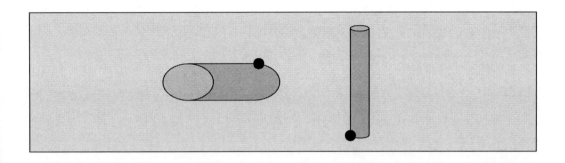

A

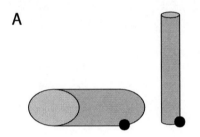

B

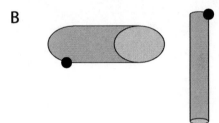

C

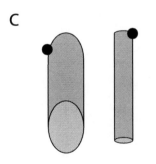

D

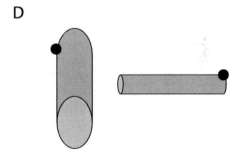

Answer

Question 16

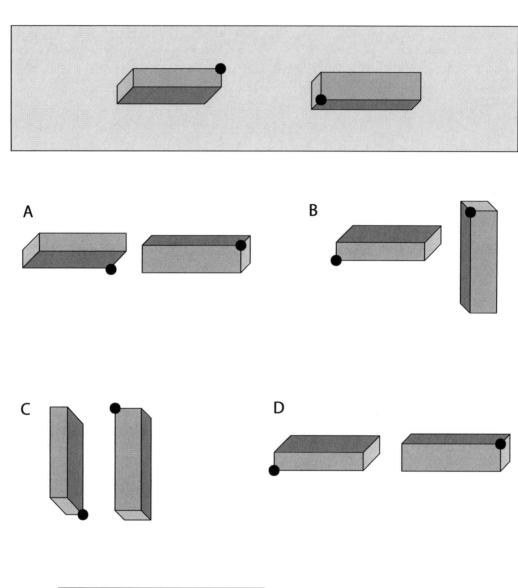

Answer

Question 17

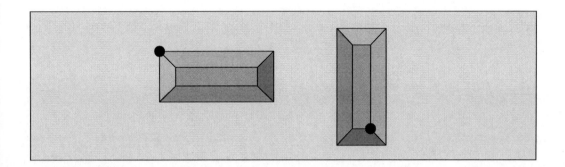

A

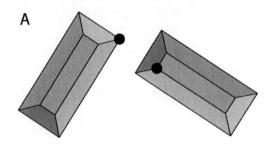

B

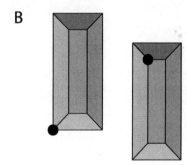

C

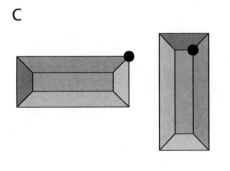

D

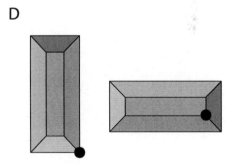

Answer [   ]

Question 18

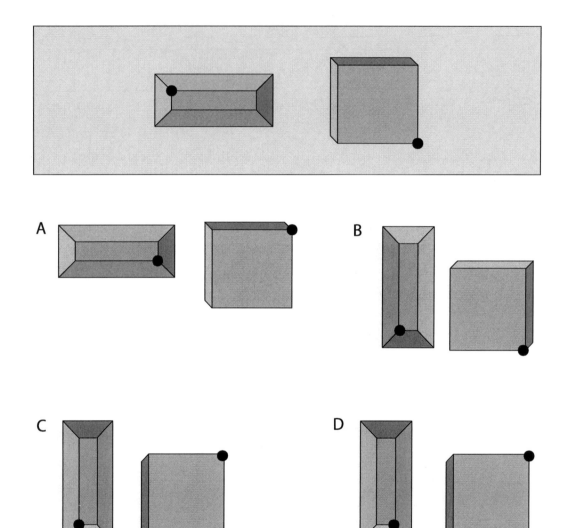

Answer [   ]

Question 19

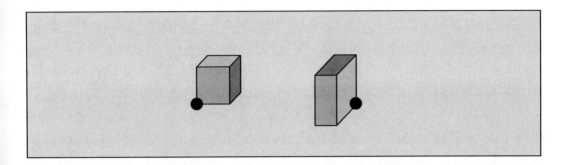

A

B

C

D

Answer

Question 20

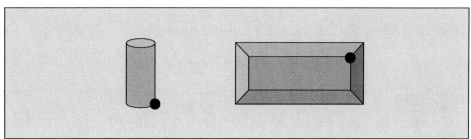

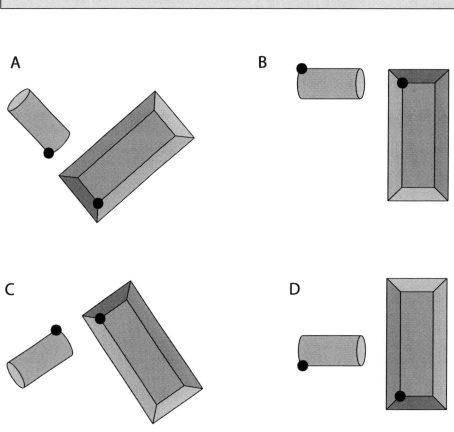

Answer

Question 21

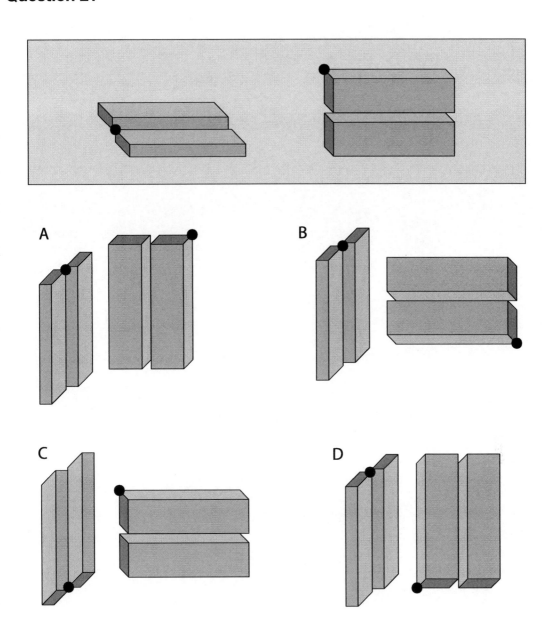

A

B

C

D

Answer

Question 22

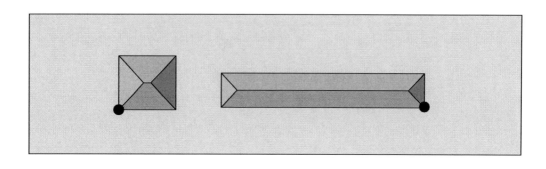

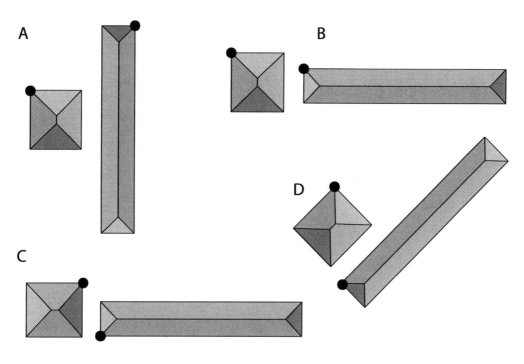

Answer [   ]

Question 23

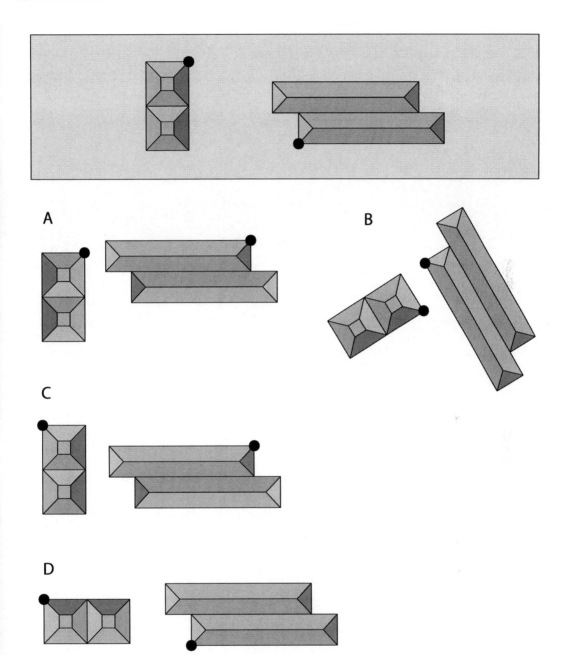

A

B

C

D

Answer

Question 24

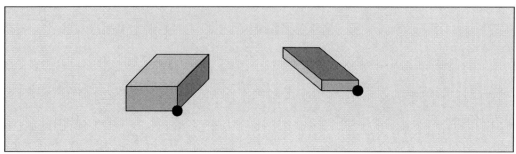

A

B

C

D

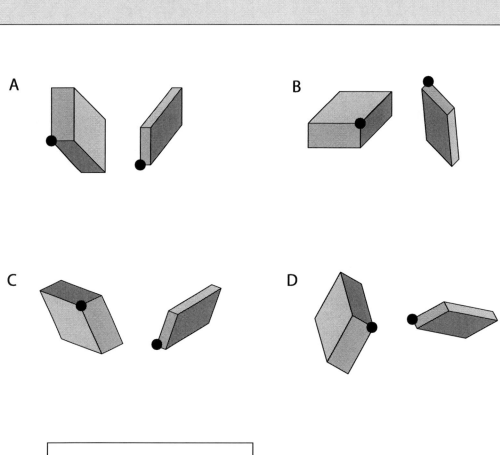

Answer

Question 25

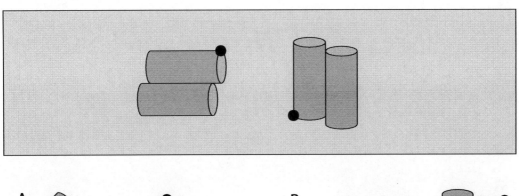

A
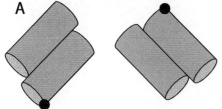

B
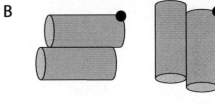

C
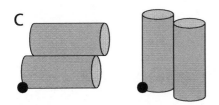

D
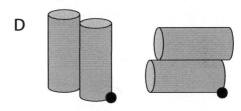

Answer [   ]

Question 26

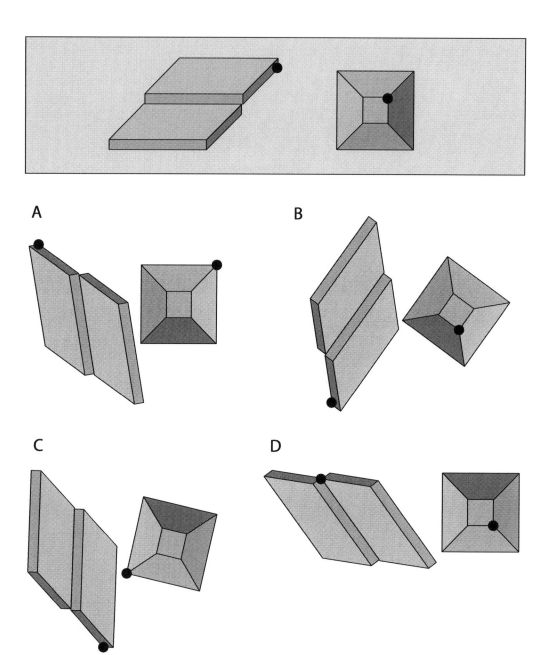

Answer

Question 27

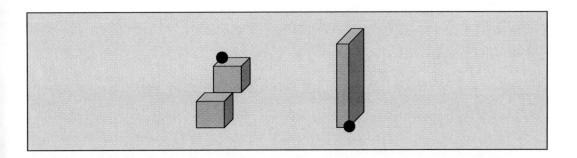

A

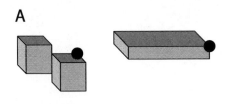

B

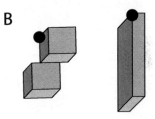

C

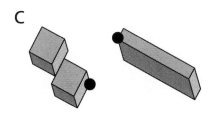

D

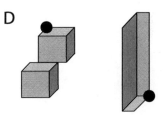

Answer

Question 28

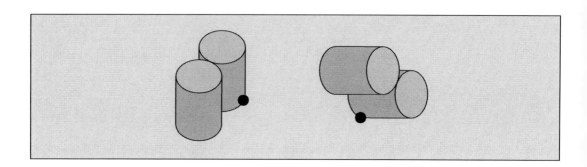

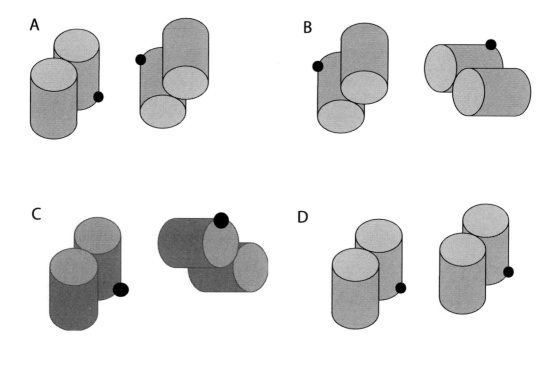

Answer [   ]

Question 29

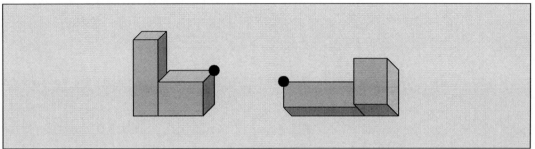

A

B

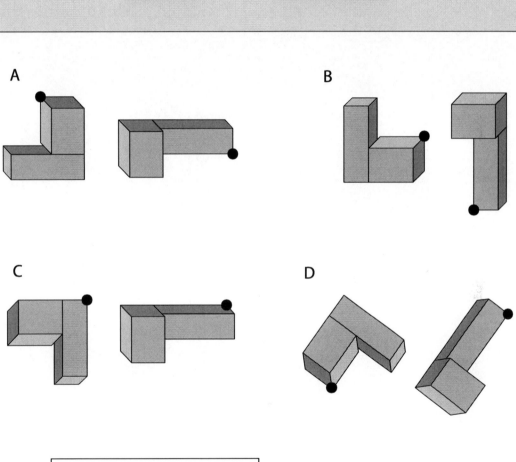

C

D

Answer

Question 30

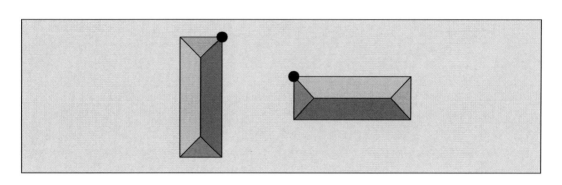

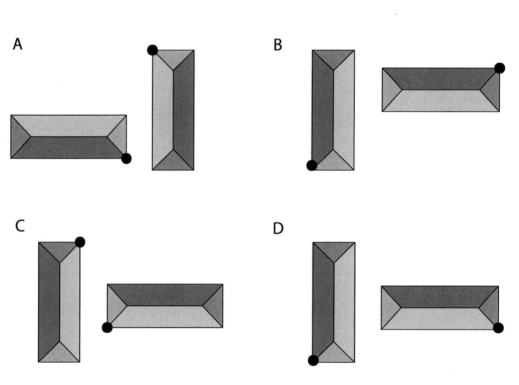

Answer

Question 31

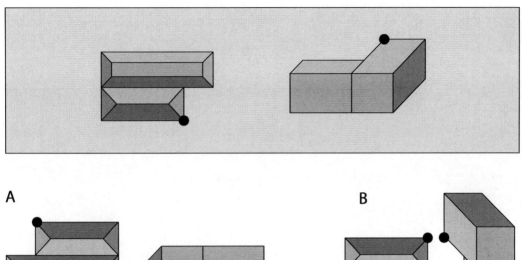

A

B

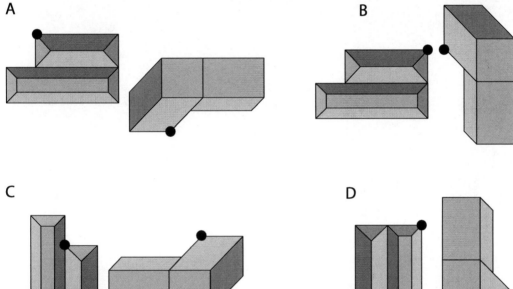

C

D

Answer

Question 32

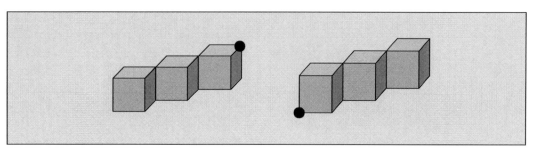

A

B

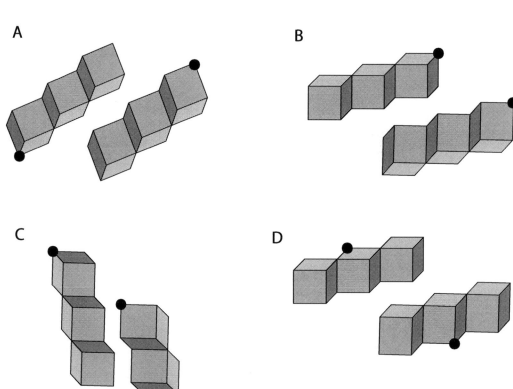

C

D

Answer

Question 33

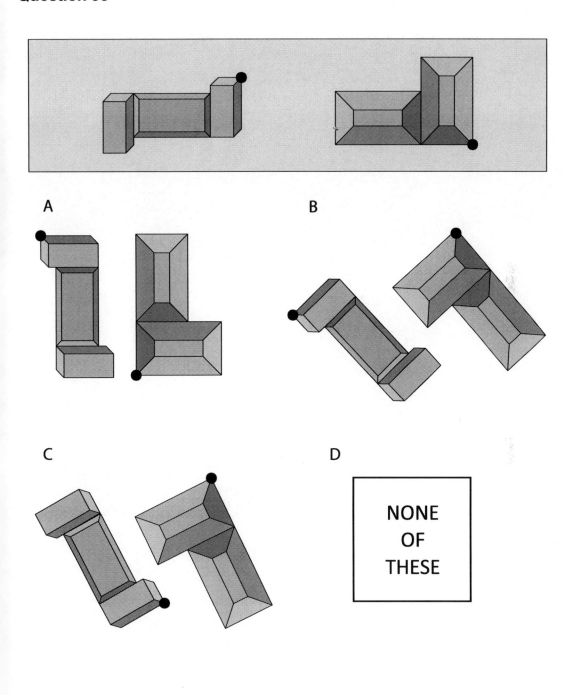

A

B

C

D

NONE
OF
THESE

Answer

Question 34

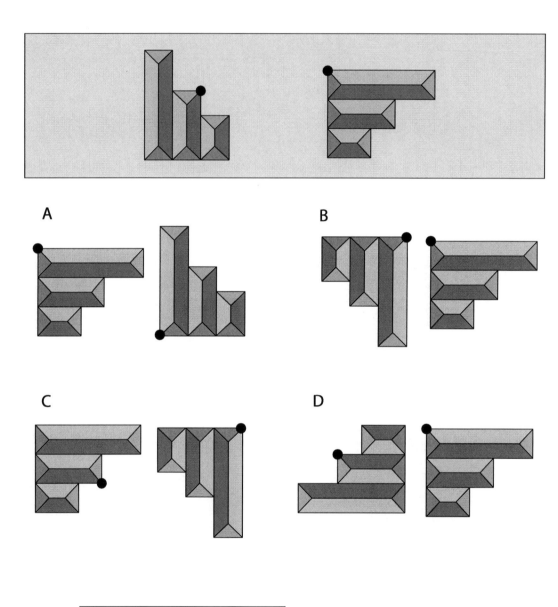

A

B

C

D

Answer

Question 35

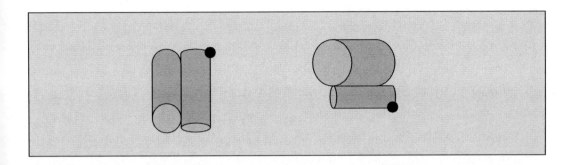

A

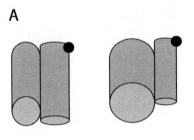

B

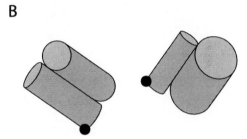

C

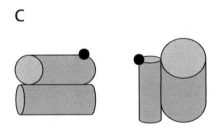

D

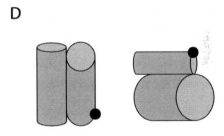

Answer [   ]

Question 36

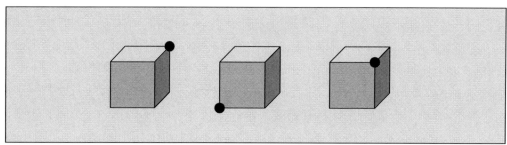

A

B

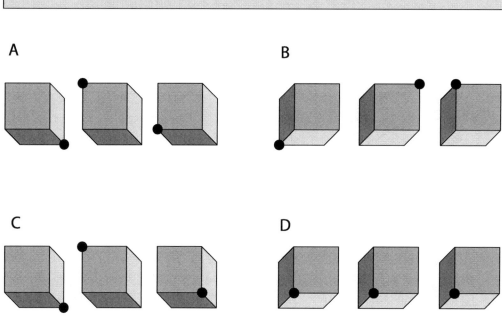

C

D

Answer

Question 37

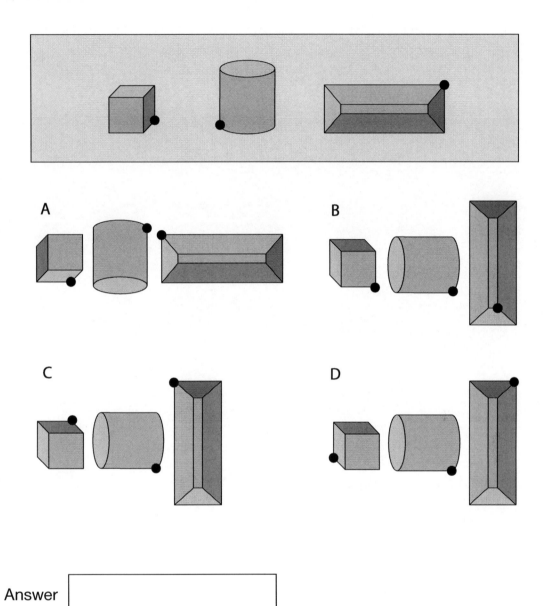

Answer [   ]

Question 38

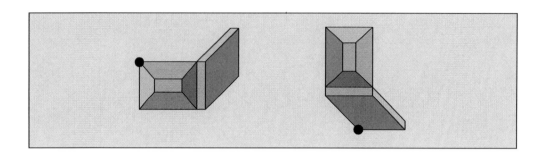

A
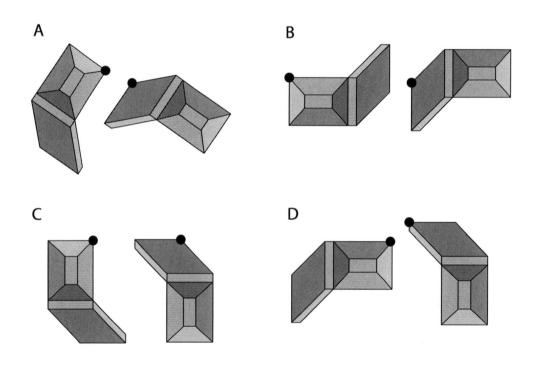

B

C

D

Answer [   ]

Question 39

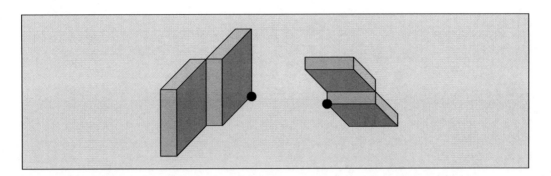

A

B

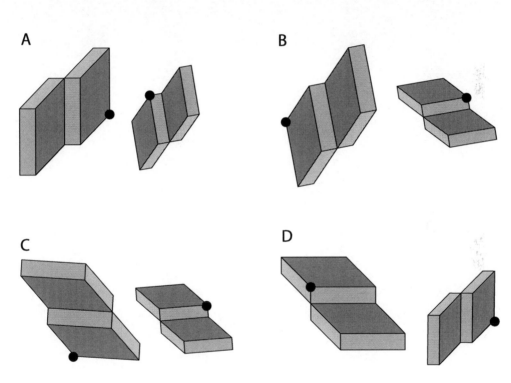

C

D

Answer

Question 40

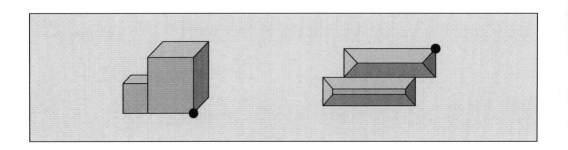

A

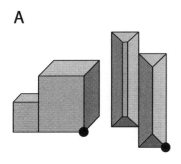

B

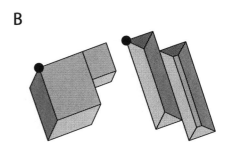

C

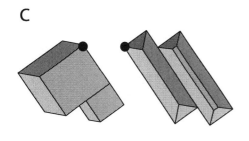

D

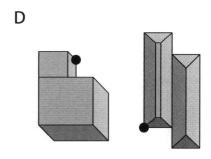

Answer

ANSWERS TO SPATIAL REASONING TEST EXERCISE 2

Q1. B

Q2. C

Q3. C

Q4. C

Q5. A

Q6. B

Q7. B

Q8. C

Q9. B

Q10. A

Q11. C

Q12. B

Q13. A

Q14. D

Q15. B

Q16. D

Q17. A

Q18. C

Q19. B

Q20. C

Q21. A

Q22. D

Q23. B

Q24. A

Q25. A

Q26. B

Q27. C

Q28. B

Q29. D

Q30. D

Q31. A

Q32. A

Q33. B

Q34. C

Q35. B

Q36. C

Q37. C

Q38. A

Q39. B

Q40. C

Once you are satisfied with your answers, please move onto the next section of the guide.

SPATIAL REASONING TESTS

TESTS

SECTION 3

SPATIAL REASONING TESTS SECTION 3

During section 3 we will revisit the same questioning format as section 1. Take a look at the following 3 shapes. Note the letters on the side of each shape:

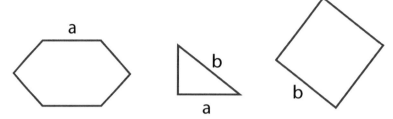

Join all of the 3 shapes together with the corresponding letters to make the following shape:

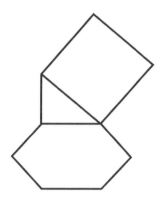

During the following spatial reasoning exercise your task is to look at the given shapes and decide which of the examples match the shape when joined together by the corresponding letters. We will now reduce the time limit for this version of the test. You have 20 minutes to answer the 40 questions.

SPATIAL REASONING TEST EXERCISE 3

Question 1

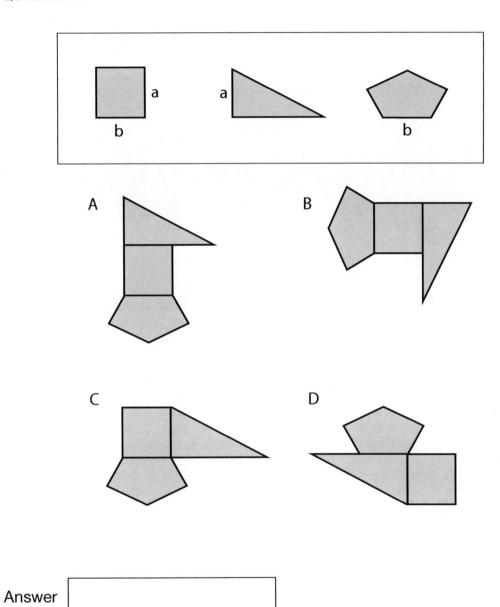

Answer [   ]

Question 2

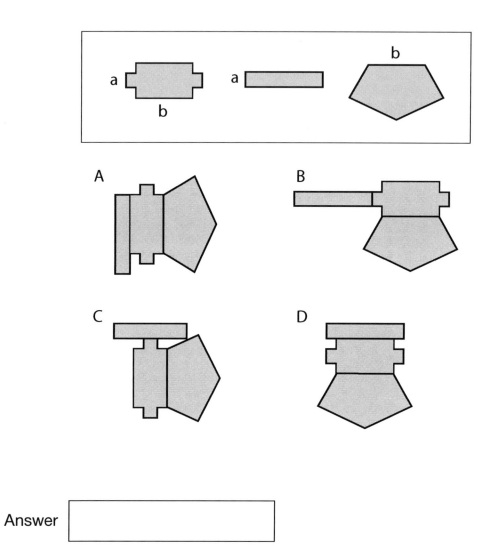

Answer

Question 3

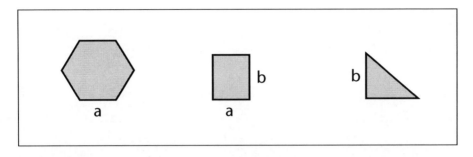

A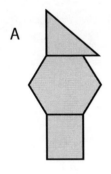

B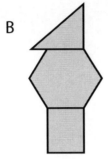

C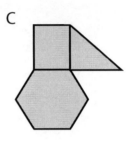

D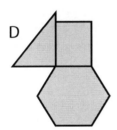

Answer

Question 4

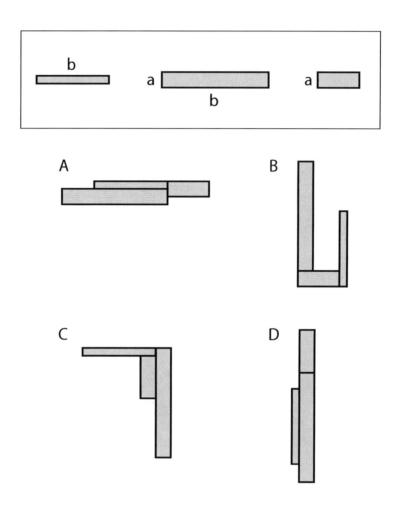

Answer

Question 5

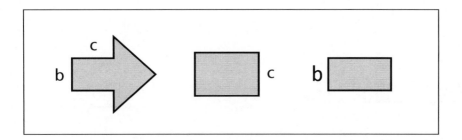

A

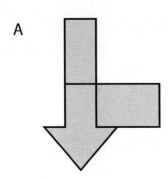

B

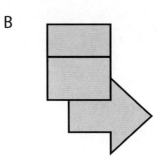

C

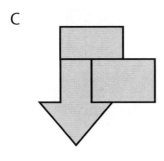

D

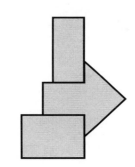

Answer

Question 6

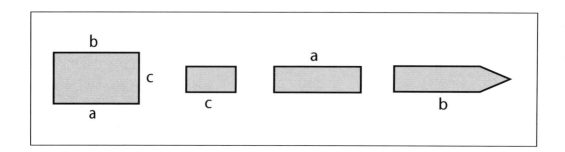

A

B

C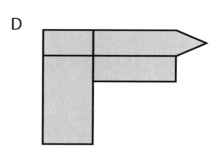

D

Answer

Question 7

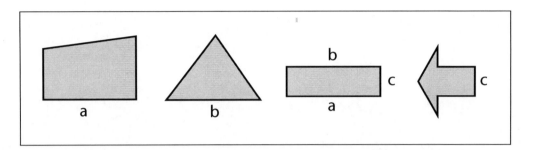

A

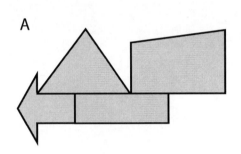

B

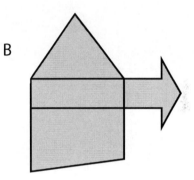

C

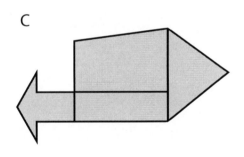

D

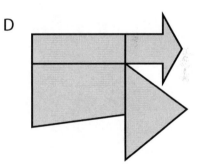

Answer

Question 8

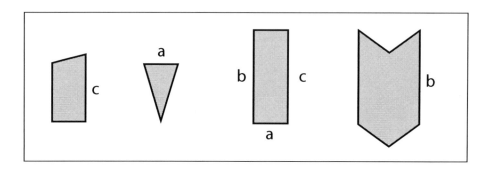

A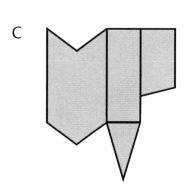

B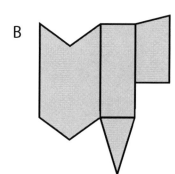

C

D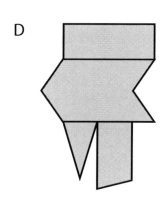

Answer

Question 9

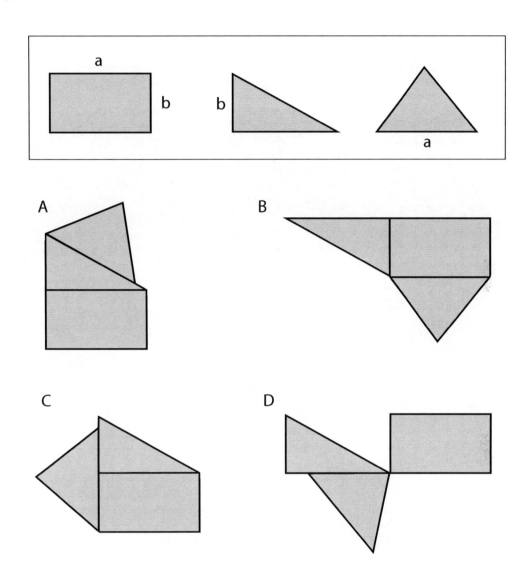

Answer

Question 10

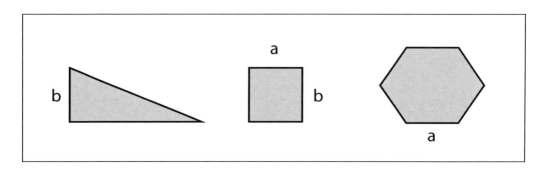

A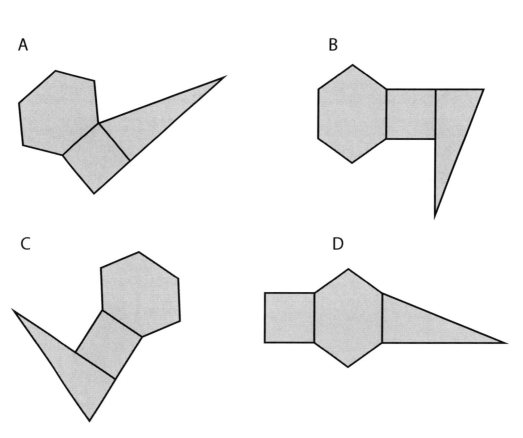

B

C

D

Answer

Question 11

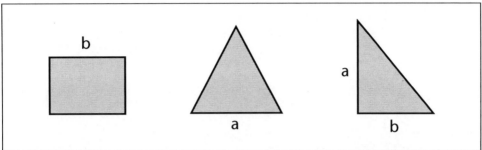

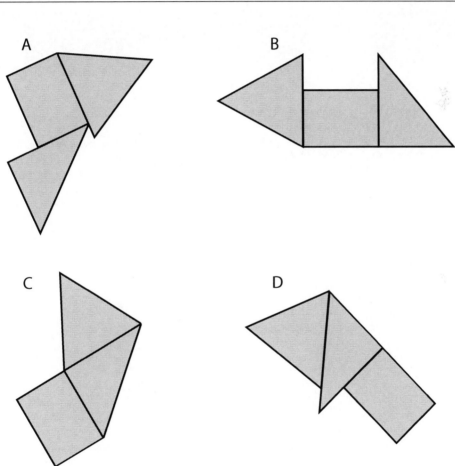

Answer

Question 12

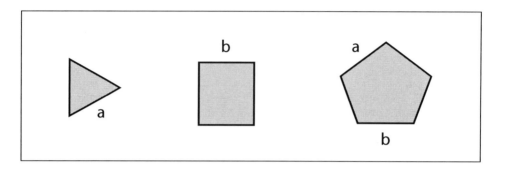

A

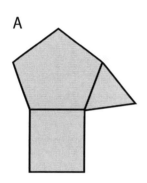

B

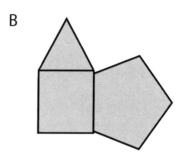

C

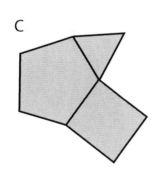

D

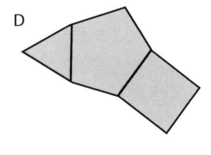

Answer

Question 13

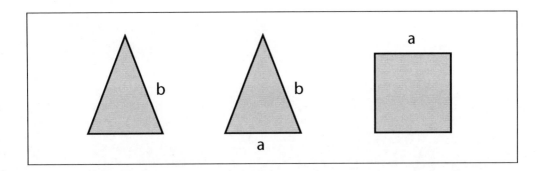

A

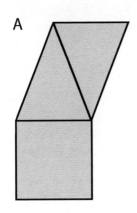

B

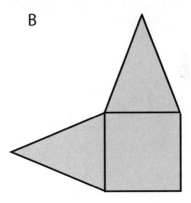

C

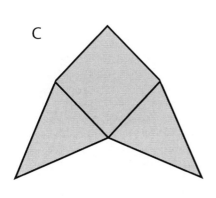

D

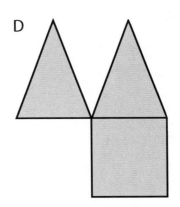

Answer

Question 14

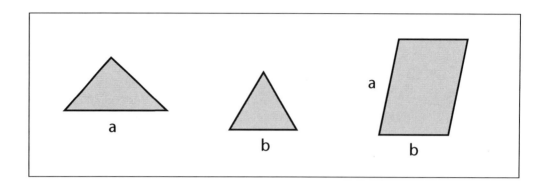

A

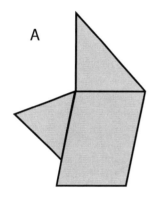

B

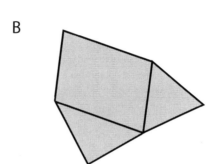

C

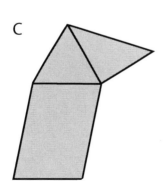

D

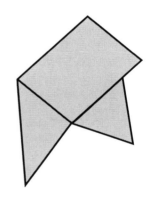

Answer

Question 15

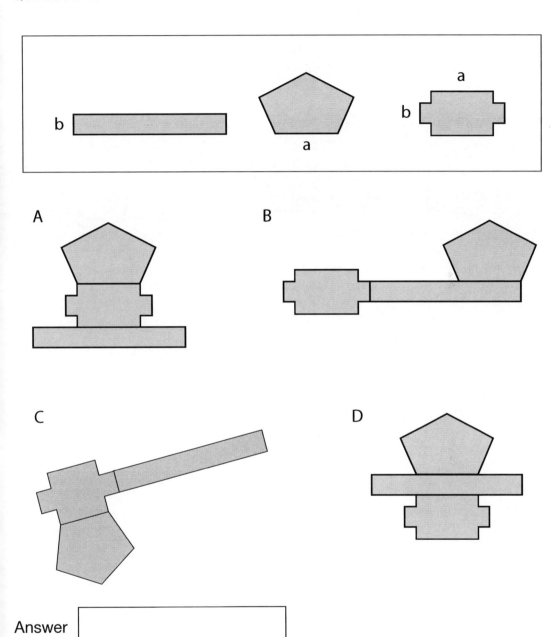

A

B

C

D

Answer

Question 16

a

b
a

b
b

A

B

C

D

Answer

Question 17

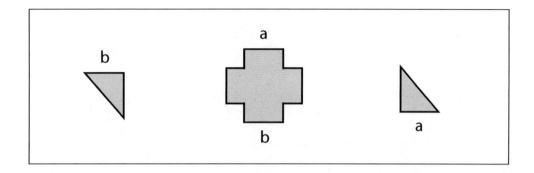

A

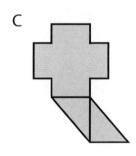

B

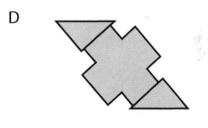

C

D

Answer

Question 18

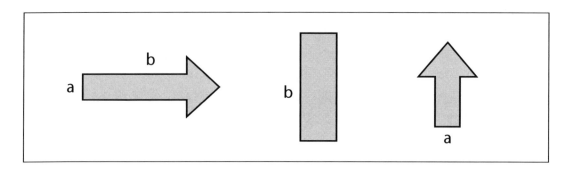

A

B

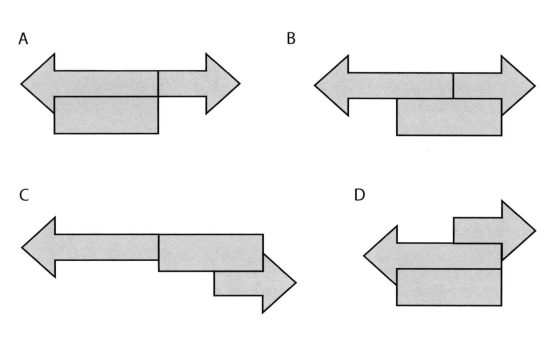

C

D

Answer [   ]

Question 19

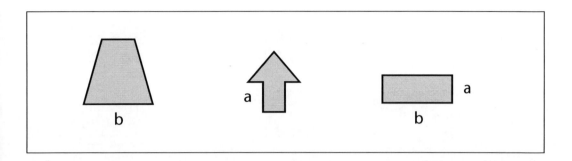

A

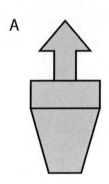

B

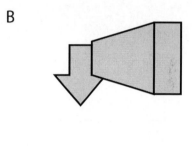

C

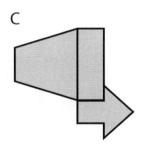

D

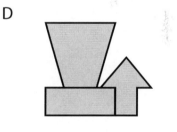

Answer

Question 20

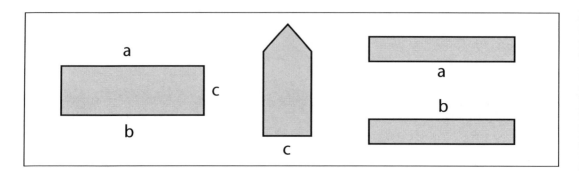

A 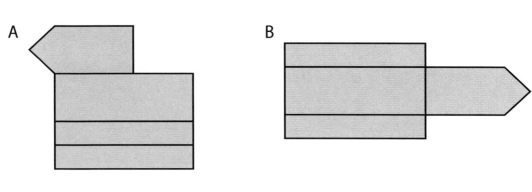 B

C 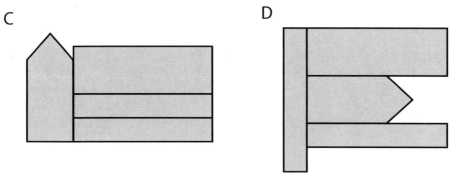 D

Answer

Question 21

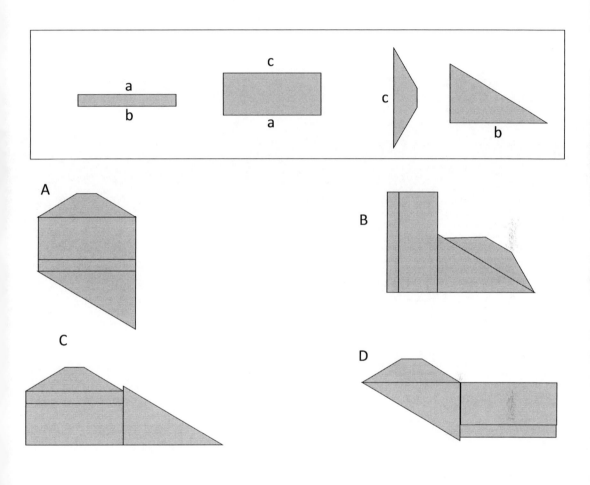

Answer

Question 22

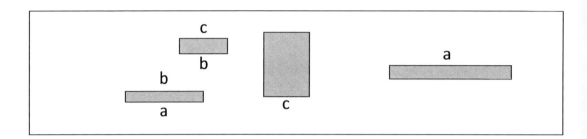

A

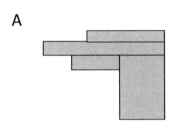

B

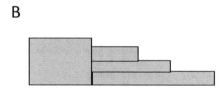

C

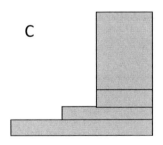

D

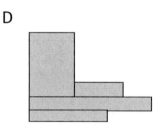

Answer

Question 23

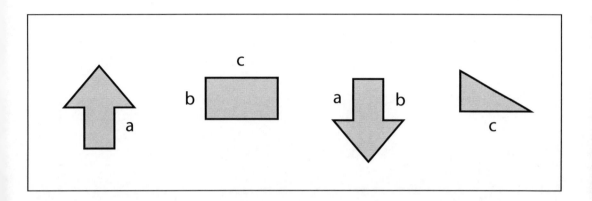

A

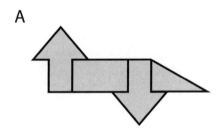

B

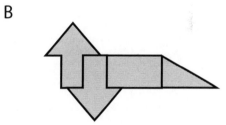

C

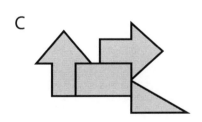

D

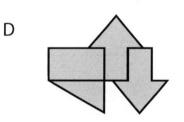

Answer

Question 24

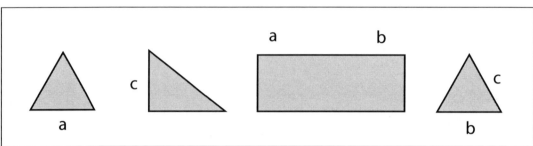

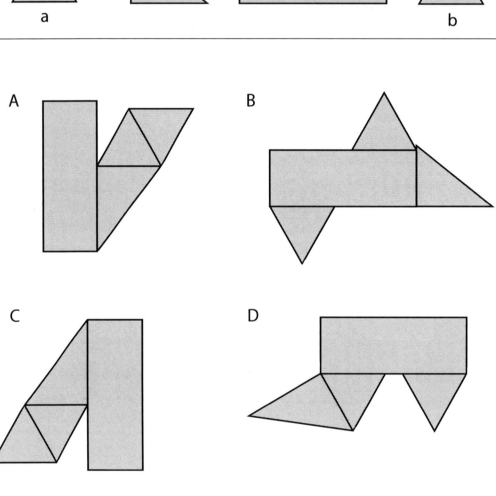

Answer [   ]

Question 25

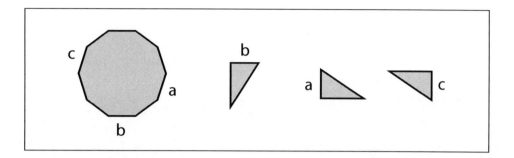

A

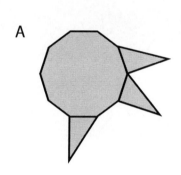

B

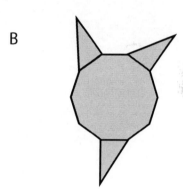

C

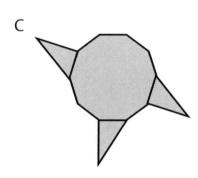

D

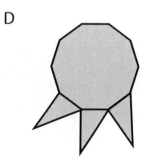

Answer

Question 26

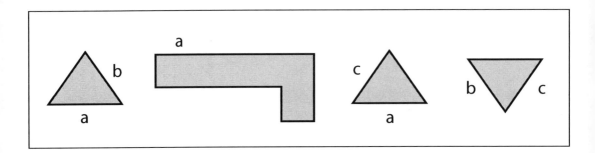

A

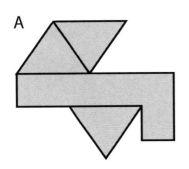

B

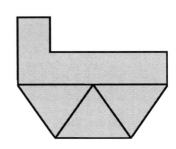

C

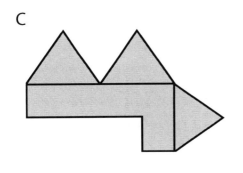

D

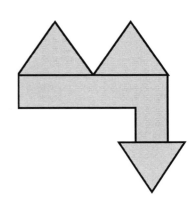

Answer

Question 27

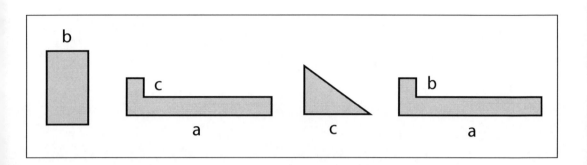

A

B

C

D

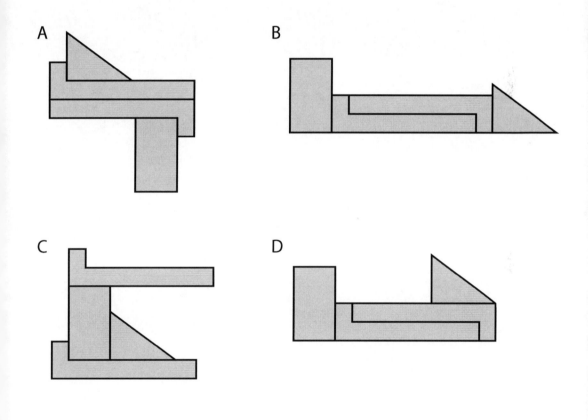

Answer

Question 28

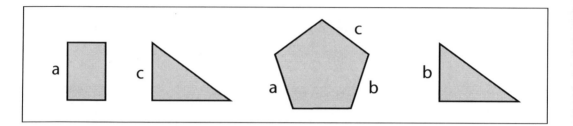

A

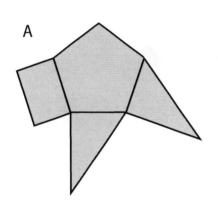

B

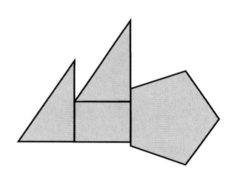

C

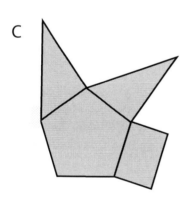

D

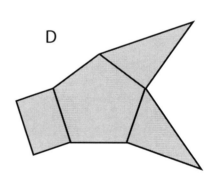

Answer [   ]

Question 29

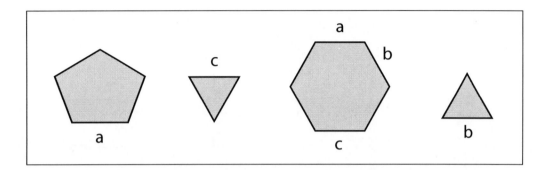

A

B

C

D

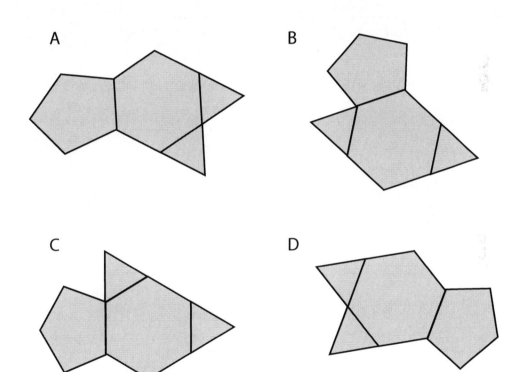

Answer

Question 30

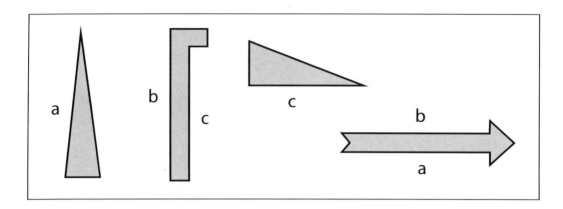

A
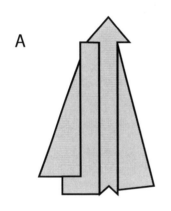

B
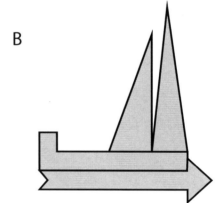

C
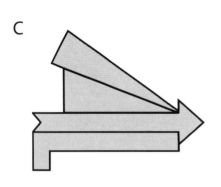

D
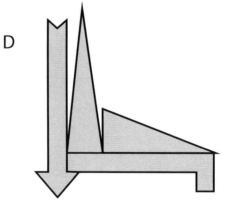

Answer

Question 31

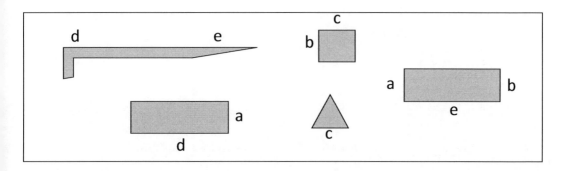

A 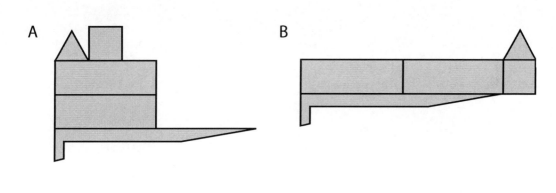 B

C 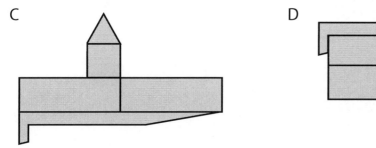 D

Answer

Question 32

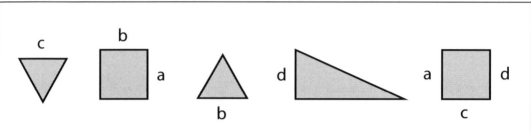

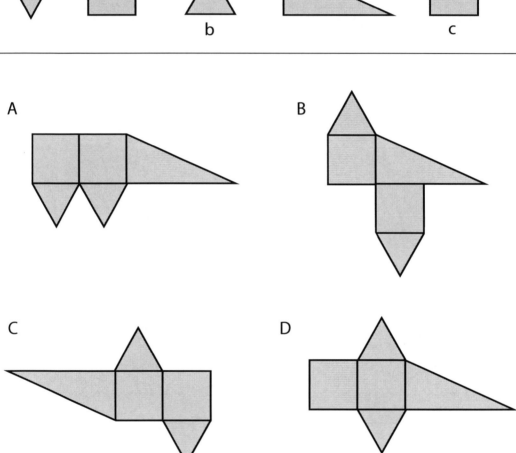

Answer [   ]

Question 33

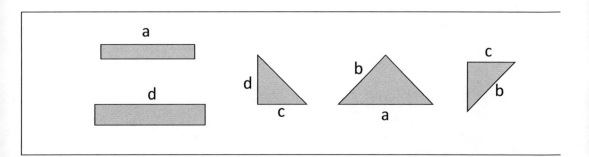

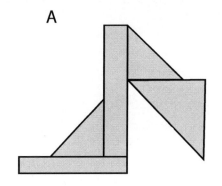

A

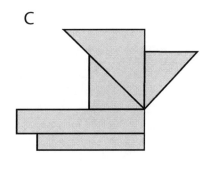

B

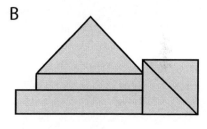

C

D

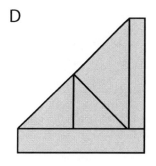

Answer

Question 34

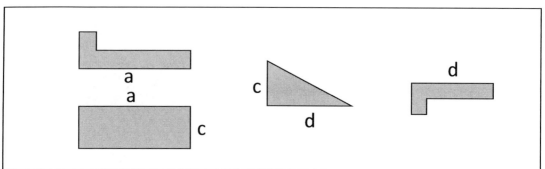

A

B

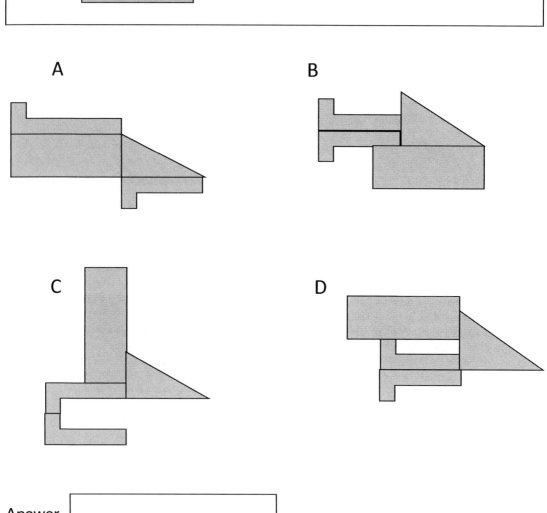

C

D

Answer

Question 35

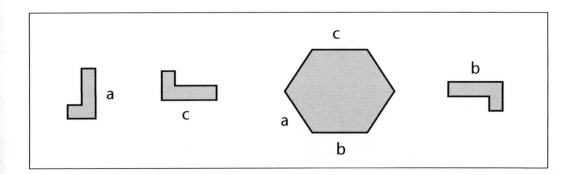

A
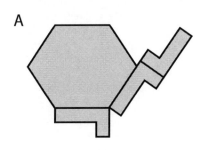

B
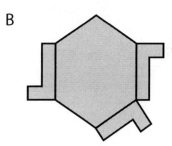

C
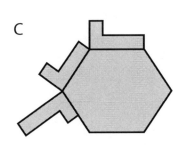

D
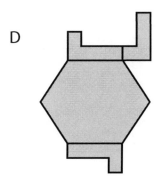

Answer

Question 36

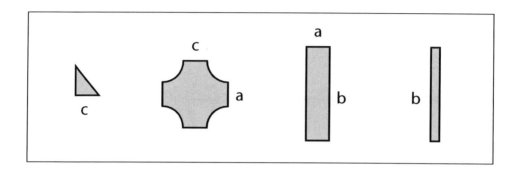

A

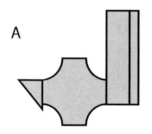

B

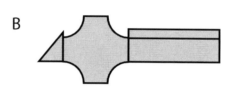

C

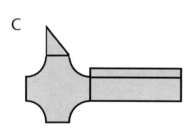

D

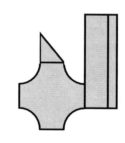

Answer

Question 37

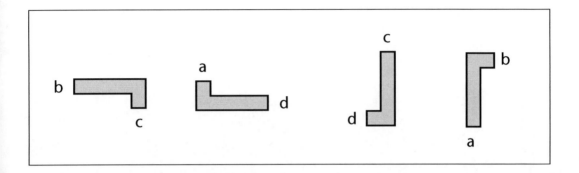

A
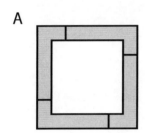

B
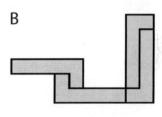

C
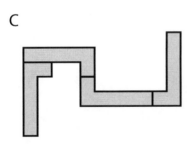

D
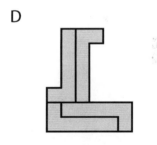

Answer

Question 38

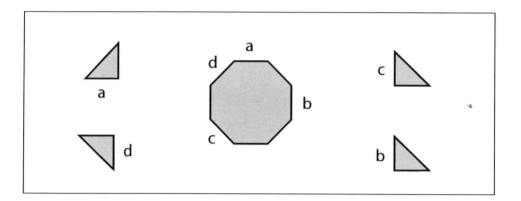

A

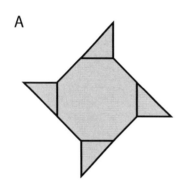

B

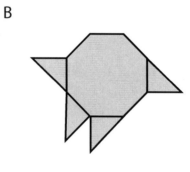

C

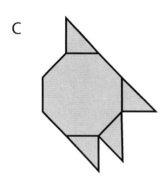

D

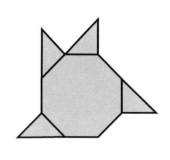

Answer [   ]

Question 39

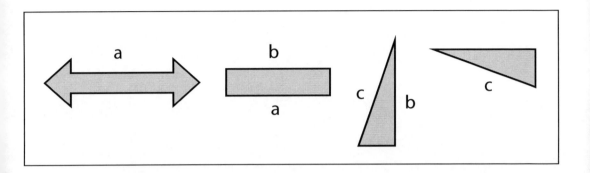

A

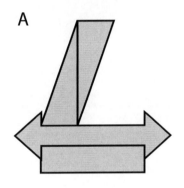

B

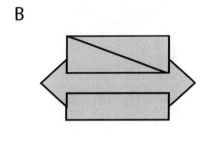

C

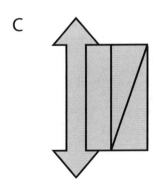

D

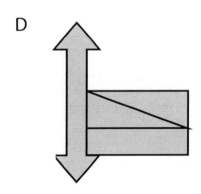

Answer

Question 40

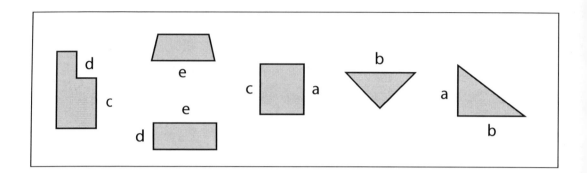

A

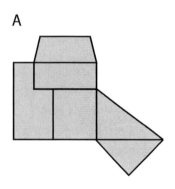

B

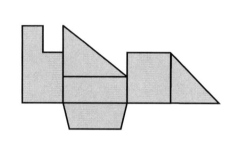

C

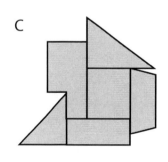

D

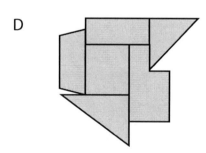

Answer

ANSWERS TO SPATIAL REASONING TEST EXERCISE 3

Q1. C

Q2. B

Q3. C

Q4. D

Q5. A

Q6. A

Q7. B

Q8. C

Q9. B

Q10. A

Q11. C

Q12. D

Q13. A

Q14. B

Q15. C

Q16. A

Q17. D

Q18. A

Q19. C

Q20. B

Q21. A

Q22. C

Q23. D

Q24. D

Q25. C

Q26. B

Q27. A

Q28. D

Q29. C

Q30. A

Q31. B

Q32. C

Q33. D

Q34. A

Q35. B

Q36. C

Q37. A

Q38. D

Q39. C

Q40. A

Once you are satisfied with your answers, please move onto the next section of the guide.

SPATIAL REASONING TESTS

TESTS

SECTION 4

SPATIAL REASONING TESTS SECTION 4

In spatial reasoning exercise 4 you need to identify which of the 4 figures presented (A, B, C or D) is identical to the first. Take a look at the following sample question:

Sample question

Which of the 4 figures presented (A, B, C or D) is identical to the first?

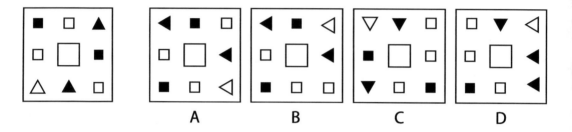

A   B   C   D

You will notice that the only shape from the 4 presented (A, B, C or D), shape A is identical to the first one when rotated either way.

You now have 40 minutes to answer the 40 questions that follow.

SPATIAL REASONING TEST EXERCISE 4

Q1. Which of the 4 figures presented (A, B, C or D) is identical to the first

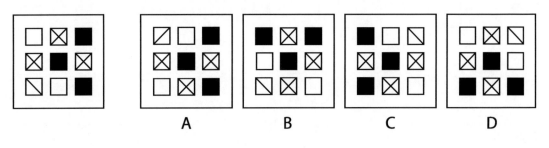

Answer:

Q2. Which of the 4 figures presented (A, B, C or D) is identical to the first?

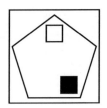 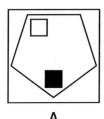 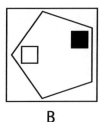 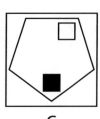 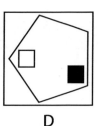

Answer:

Q3. Which of the 4 figures presented (A, B, C or D) is identical to the first?

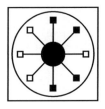 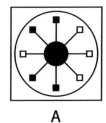 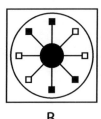 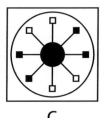 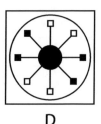

Answer:

Q4. Which of the 4 figures presented (A, B, C or D) is identical to the first?

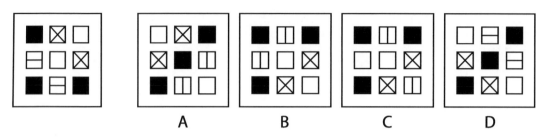

A   B   C   D

Answer: [   ]

Q5. Which of the 4 figures presented (A, B, C or D) is identical to the first?

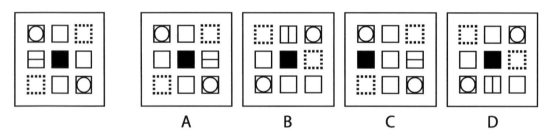

A   B   C   D

Answer: [   ]

Q6. Which of the 4 figures presented (A, B, C or D) is identical to the first?

 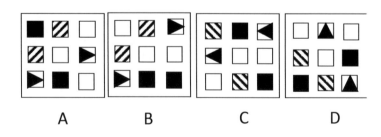

A   B   C   D

Answer: [   ]

Q7. Which of the 4 figures presented (A, B, C or D) is identical to the first?

A   B   C   D

Answer:

Q8. Which of the 4 figures presented (A, B, C or D) is identical to the first?

A   B   C   D

Answer:

Q9. Which of the 4 figures presented (A, B, C or D) is identical to the first?

A   B   C   D

Answer:

Q10. Which of the 4 figures presented (A, B, C or D) is identical to the first?

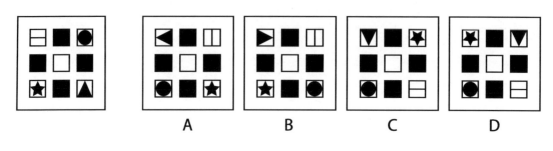

Answer: [ ]

Q11. Which of the 4 figures presented (A, B, C or D) is identical to the first?

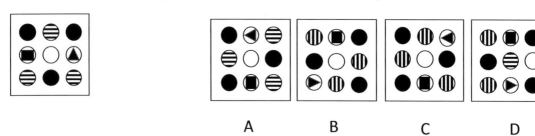

Answer: [ ]

Q12. Which of the 4 figures presented (A, B, C or D) is identical to the first?

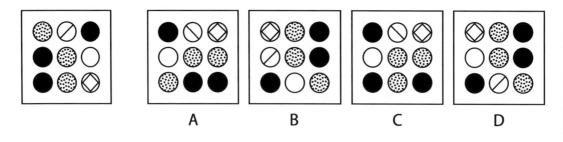

Answer: [ ]

Q13. Which of the 4 figures presented (A, B, C or D) is identical to the first?

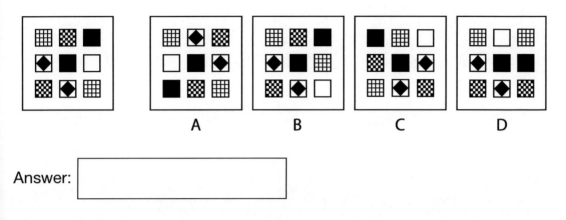

Answer:

Q14. Which of the 4 figures presented (A, B, C or D) is identical to the first?

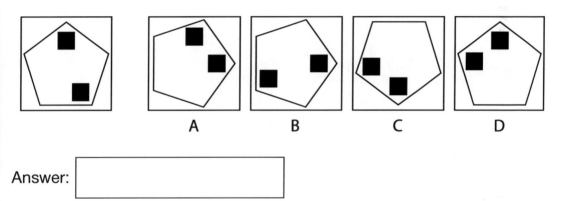

Answer:

Q15. Which of the 4 figures presented (A, B, C or D) is identical to the first?

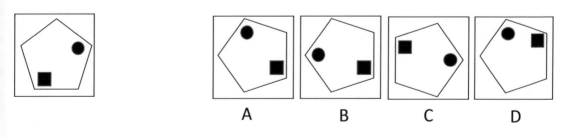

Answer:

Q16. Which of the 4 figures presented (A, B, C or D) is identical to the first?

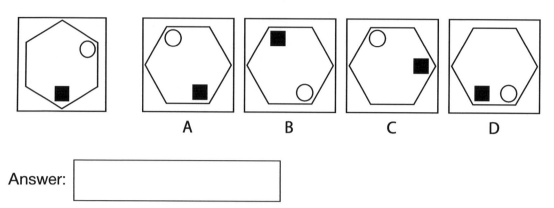

Answer:

Q17. Which of the 4 figures presented (A, B, C or D) is identical to the first?

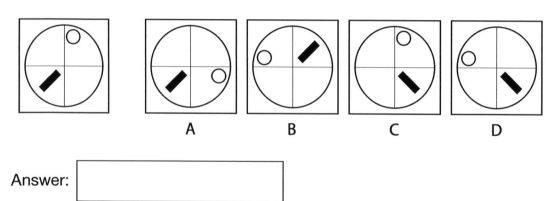

Answer:

Q18. Which of the 4 figures presented (A, B, C or D) is identical to the first?

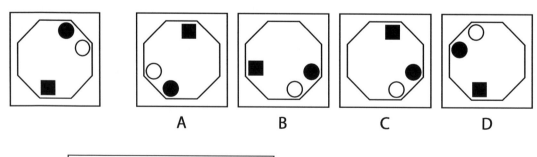

Answer:

Q19. Which of the 4 figures presented (A, B, C or D) is identical to the first?

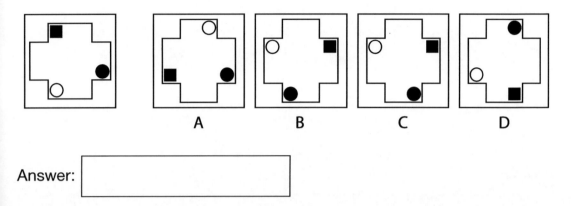

Answer:

Q20. Which of the 4 figures presented (A, B, C or D) is identical to the first?

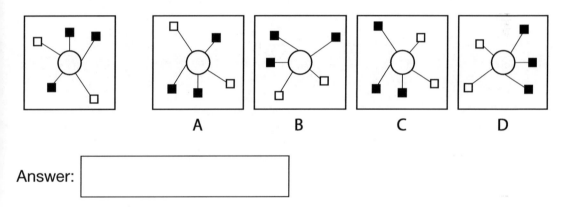

Answer:

Q21. Which of the 4 figures presented (A, B, C or D) is identical to the first?

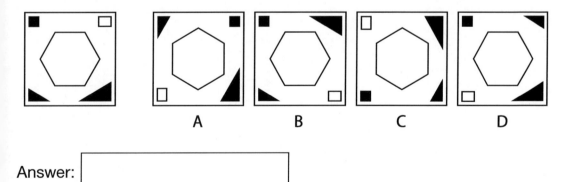

Answer:

Q22. Which of the 4 figures presented (A, B, C or D) is identical to the first?

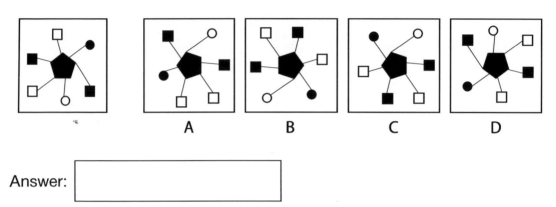

Answer:

Q23. Which of the 4 figures presented (A, B, C or D) is identical to the first?

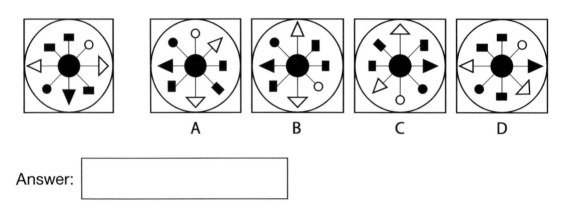

Answer:

Q24. Which of the 4 figures presented (A, B, C or D) is identical to the first?

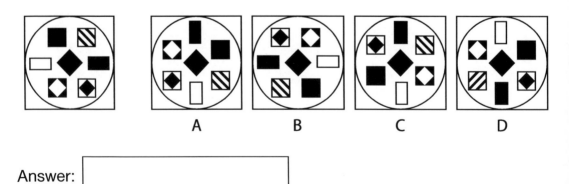

Answer:

Q25. Which of the 4 figures presented (A, B, C or D) is identical to the first?

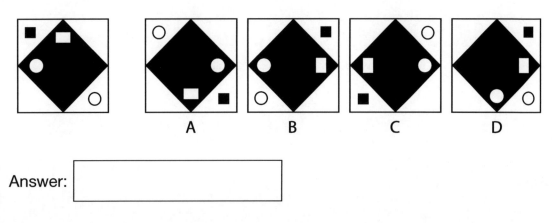

Q26. Which of the 4 figures presented (A, B, C or D) is identical to the first?

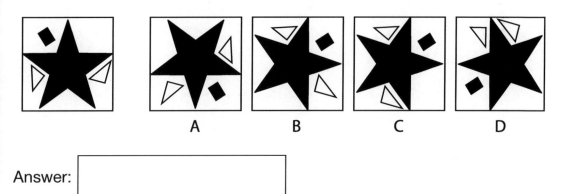

Q27. Which of the 4 figures presented (A, B, C or D) is identical to the first?

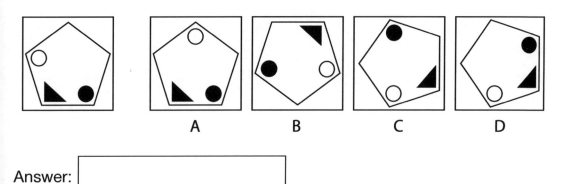

Answer:

Q28. Which of the 4 figures presented (A, B, C or D) is identical to the first?

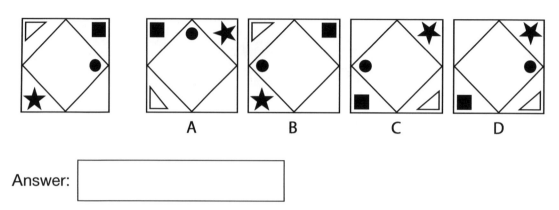

Answer:

Q29. Which of the 4 figures presented (A, B, C or D) is identical to the first?

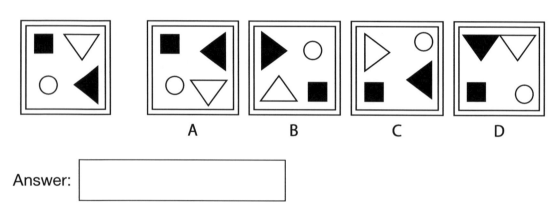

Answer:

Q30. Which of the 4 figures presented (A, B, C or D) is identical to the first?

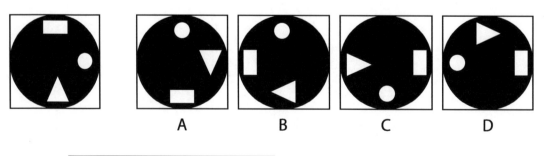

Answer:

Q31. Which of the 4 figures presented (A, B, C or D) is identical to the first?

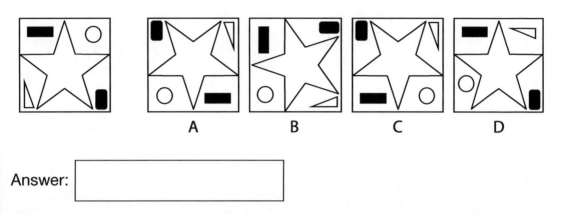

A   B   C   D

Answer:

Q32. Which of the 4 figures presented (A, B, C or D) is identical to the first?

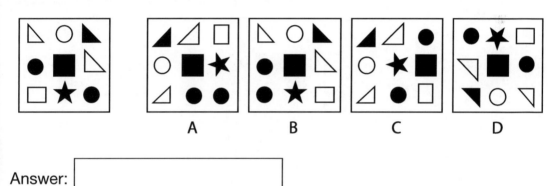

A   B   C   D

Answer:

Q33. Which of the 4 figures presented (A, B, C or D) is identical to the first?

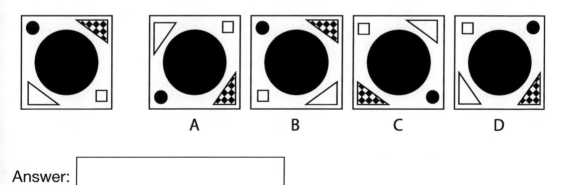

A   B   C   D

Answer:

Q34. Which of the 4 figures presented (A, B, C or D) is identical to the first?

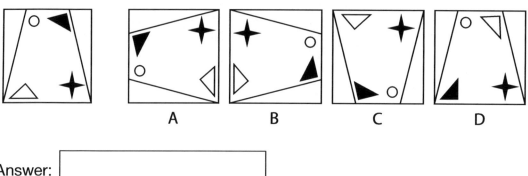

Answer: [   ]

Q35. Which of the 4 figures presented (A, B, C or D) is identical to the first?

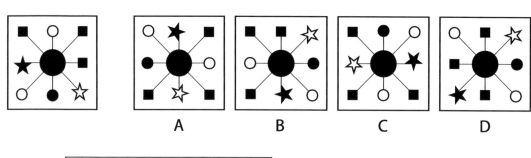

Answer: [   ]

Q36. Which of the 4 figures presented (A, B, C or D) is identical to the first?

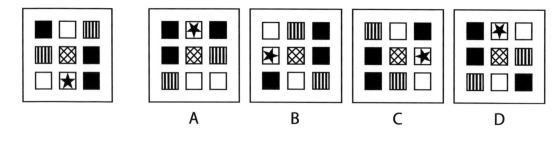

Answer: [   ]

Q37. Which of the 4 figures presented (A, B, C or D) is identical to the first?

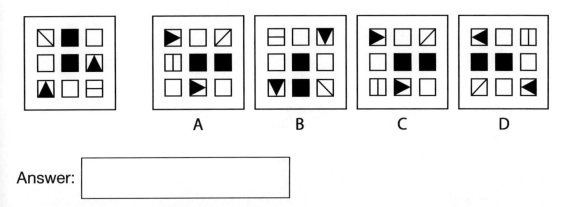

Answer:

Q38. Which of the 4 figures presented (A, B, C or D) is identical to the first?

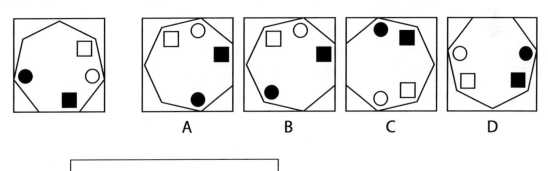

Answer:

Q39. Which of the 4 figures presented (A, B, C or D) is identical to the first?

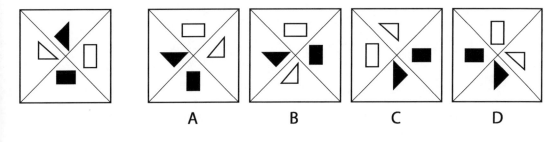

Answer:

Q40. Which of the 4 figures presented (A, B, C or D) is identical to the first?

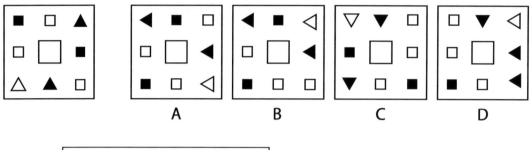

Answer:

Once you have completed the test please check your answers carefully.

ANSWERS TO SPATIAL REASONING TEST EXERCISE 4

Q1. C

Q2. B

Q3. A

Q4. B

Q5. A

Q6. C

Q7. A

Q8. D

Q9. B

Q10. C

Q11. A

Q12. D

Q13. A

Q14. B

Q15. A

Q16. C

Q17. D

Q18. A

Q19. B

Q20. A

Q21. C

Q22. D

Q23. B

Q24. B

Q25. A

Q26. C

Q27. D

Q28. C

Q29. B

Q30. C

Q31. A

Q32. D

Q33. C

Q34. A

Q35. B

Q36. D

Q37. C

Q38. A

Q39. B

Q40. A

Once you are satisfied with your answers, please move onto the next section of the guide.

SPATIAL REASONING TESTS

TESTS

SECTION 5

SPATIAL REASONING TESTS SECTION 5

In this section of the guide you will be required to identify which shapes in a particular group correspond with shapes from a second group. This type of spatial reasoning test assesses both speed and accuracy with regards to your ability to visually match shapes under timed conditions. Take a look at the following sample question:

Q. Which shape in Group 2 corresponds to the shape in Group 1?

Group 1   Group 2

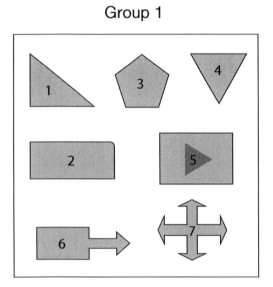 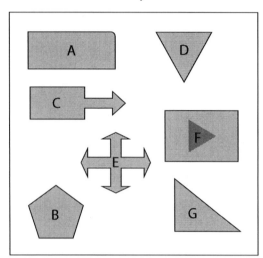

You will notice that shape A in Group 2 corresponds with shape 2 in Group 1. The correct answers to the remaining shapes are as follows:

A = 2

B = 3

C = 6

D = 4

E = 7

F = 5

G = 1

Now try the following test. There are 10 questions and you just have 5 minutes to complete the test.

SPATIAL REASONING TEST EXERCISE 5

Q1. Which shape in Group 2 corresponds to the shape in Group 1?

Group 1   Group 2

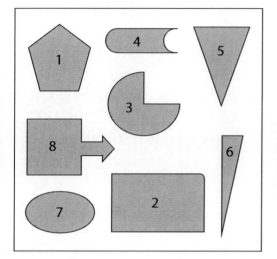 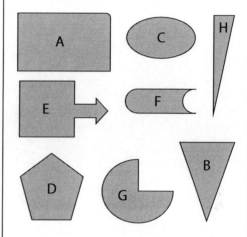

Answers:

A =

B =

C =

D =

E =

F =

G =

H =

Q2. Which shape in Group 2 corresponds to the shape in Group 1?

Group 1

Group 2

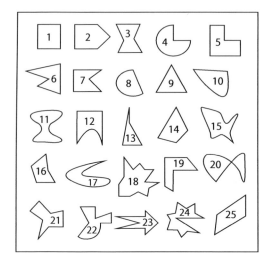

Answers:

B =

C =

E =

I =

J =

K =

L =

O =

S =

T =

U =

W =

Q3. Which shape in Group 2 corresponds to the shape in Group 1?

Group 1

Group 2

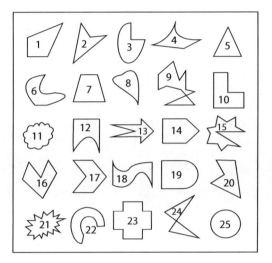

Answers:

A =

C =

D =

F =

G =

H =

I =

J =

L =

O =

Q =

W =

Q4. Which shape in Group 2 corresponds to the shape in Group 1?

Group 1

Group 2

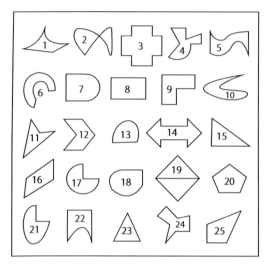

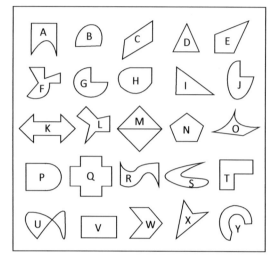

Answers:

B =

E =

F =

G =

K =

M =

O =

Q =

R =

U =

W =

Y =

Q5. Which shape in Group 2 corresponds to the shape in Group 1?

Group 1

Group 2

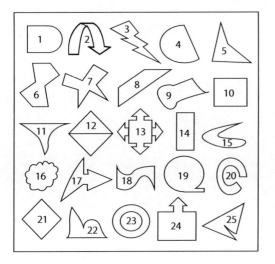

Answers:

B =

C =

E =

F =

H =

I =

L =

N =

P =

Q =

R =

Y =

Q6. Which shape in Group 2 corresponds to the shape in Group 1?

Group 1

Group 2

Answers:

A =

B =

E =

H =

J =

N =

O =

Q =

R =

U =

W =

Y =

Q7. Which shape in Group 2 corresponds to the shape in Group 1?

Group 1

Group 2

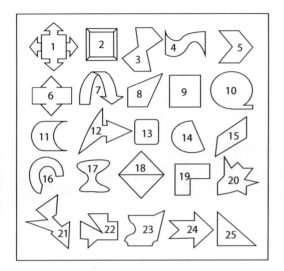

Answers:

A =

C =

D =

G =

J =

L =

O =

Q =

T =

U =

W =

X =

Q8. Which shape in Group 2 corresponds to the shape in Group 1?

Group 1   Group 2

Answers:

C =

D =

F =

G =

J =

M =

Q =

T =

U =

V =

W =

Y =

Q9. Which shape in Group 2 corresponds to the shape in Group 1?

Group 1

Group 2

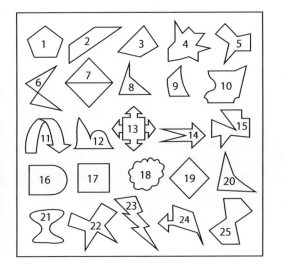

Answers:

B =

C =

G =

I =

L =

N =

P =

Q =

R =

S =

U =

V =

Q10. Which shape in Group 2 corresponds to the shape in Group 1?

Group 1

Group 2

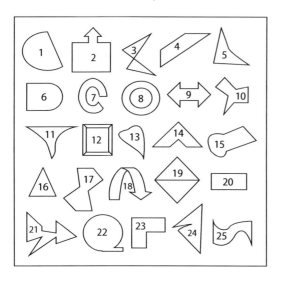 

Answers:

B =

D =

F =

H =

L =

M =

O =

Q =

T =

U =

V =

X =

Once you have completed the test, please check your answers carefully.

ANSWERS TO SPATIAL REASONING TEST EXERCISE 5

Question 1

A = 2

B = 5

C = 7

D = 1

E = 8

F = 4

G = 3

H = 6

Question 2

B = 15

C = 17

E = 12

I = 18

J = 22

K = 6

L = 20

O = 24

S = 23

T = 19

U = 4

W = 2

Question 3

A = 7

C = 15

D = 18

F = 10

G = 14

H = 22

I = 24

J = 21

L = 16

O = 2

Q = 9

W = 11

Question 4

B = 13

E = 25

F = 4

G = 17

K = 14

M = 19

O = 1

Q = 3

R = 5

U = 2

W = 12

Y = 6

Question 5

B = 24

C = 5

E = 11

F = 22

H = 18

I = 13

L = 23

N = 15

P = 25

Q = 2

R = 3

Y = 7

Question 6

A = 13

B = 9

E = 1

H = 19

J = 18

N = 24

O = 23

Q = 4

R = 14

U = 6

W = 7

Y = 11

Question 7

A = 22
C = 6
D = 8
G = 23
J = 19
L = 21
O = 20
Q = 5
T = 14
U = 7
W = 1
X = 11

Question 8

C = 23
D = 20
F = 16
G = 17
J = 18
M = 15
Q = 5
T = 1
U = 11
V = 12
W = 4
Y = 2

Question 9

B = 24

C =16

G = 18

I = 23

L = 3

N = 14

P = 12

Q = 8

R = 15

S = 10

U = 20

V = 13

Question 10

B = 21

D = 17

F = 23

H = 19

L = 14

M = 24

O = 12

Q = 10

T = 8

U = 2

V = 7

X = 6

Once you are satisfied with your answers, move on to the next section of the guide.

SPATIAL REASONING TESTS

SECTION 6

SPATIAL REASONING TESTS SECTION 6

In this next set of questions you have to identify which of the shapes presented are identical. These tests are sometimes referred to as 'visual com-
parison' tests. The aim of this test is to work as quickly and accurately as
possible. More often than not, you will lose marks for incorrect answers.
Take a look at the following question:

Q1. Which of the following 2 shapes are identical?

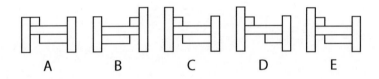

A   B   C   D   E

You will notice that shapes C + E are identical. Once you understand what
is required, work through the following exercise as quickly and accurately as
possible. There are 20 questions and you have just 4 minutes to complete
the test.

SPATIAL REASONING TEST EXERCISE 6

Q1. Which of the following 2 shapes are identical?

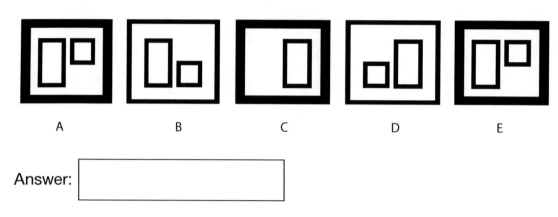

A   B   C   D   E

Answer:

Q2. Which of the following 2 shapes are identical?

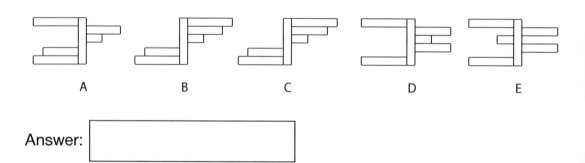

A   B   C   D   E

Answer:

Q3. Which of the following 2 shapes are identical?

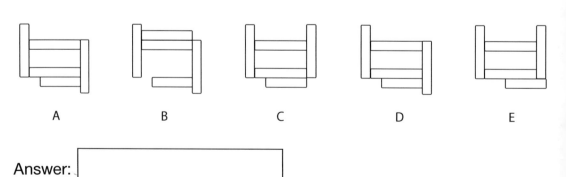

A   B   C   D   E

Answer:

Q4. Which of the following 2 shapes are identical?

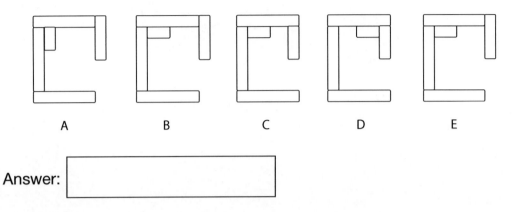

A   B   C   D   E

Answer:

Q5. Which of the following 2 shapes are identical?

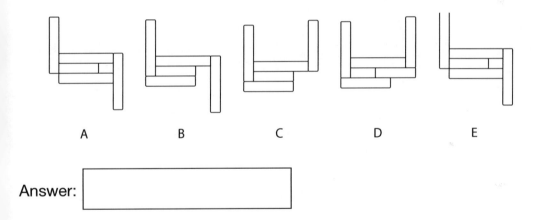

A   B   C   D   E

Answer:

Q6. Which of the following 2 shapes are identical?

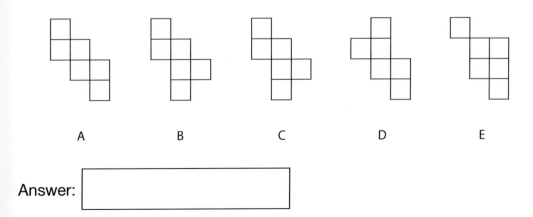

A   B   C   D   E

Answer:

Q7. Which of the following 2 shapes are identical?

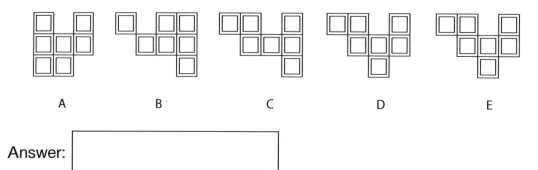

A   B   C   D   E

Answer: [   ]

Q8. Which of the following 2 shapes are identical?

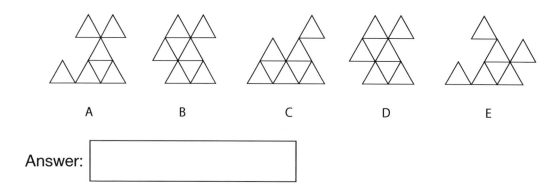

A   B   C   D   E

Answer: [   ]

Q9. Which of the following 2 shapes are identical?

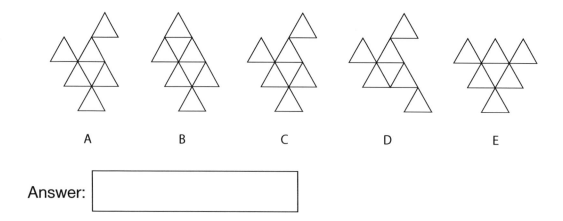

A   B   C   D   E

Answer: [   ]

Q10. Which of the following 2 shapes are identical?

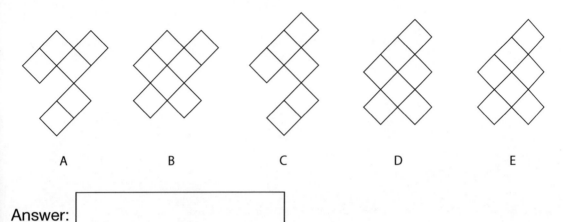

A   B   C   D   E

Answer:

Q11. Which of the following 2 shapes are identical?

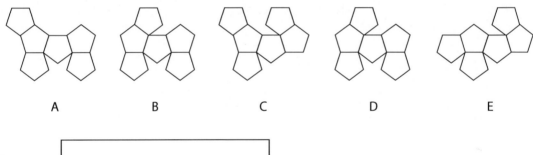

A   B   C   D   E

Answer:

Q12. Which of the following 2 shapes are identical?

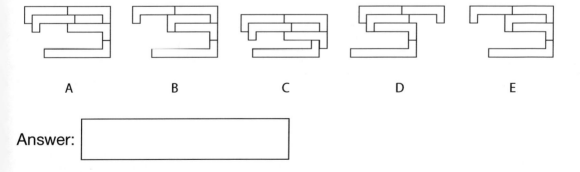

A   B   C   D   E

Answer:

Q13. Which of the following 2 shapes are identical?

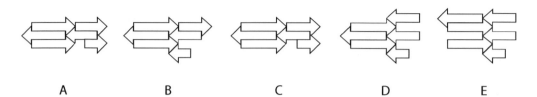

A   B   C   D   E

Answer: [   ]

Q14. Which of the following 2 shapes are identical?

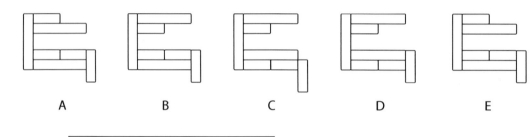

A   B   C   D   E

Answer: [   ]

Q15. Which of the following 2 shapes are identical?

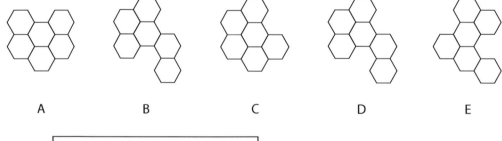

A   B   C   D   E

Answer: [   ]

Q16. Which of the following 2 shapes are identical?

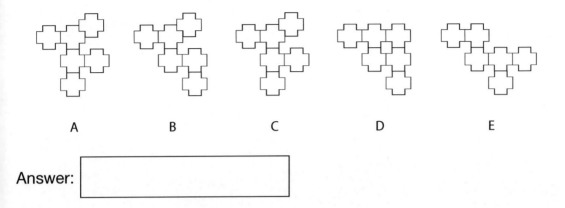

A   B   C   D   E

Answer:

Q17. Which of the following 2 shapes are identical?

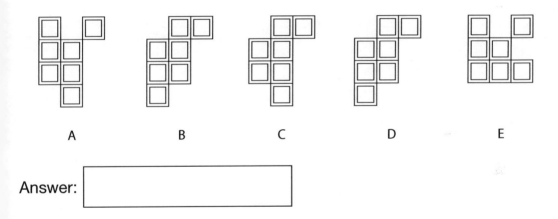

A   B   C   D   E

Answer:

Q18. Which of the following 2 shapes are identical?

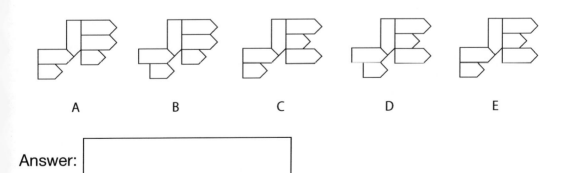

A   B   C   D   E

Answer:

Q19. Which of the following 2 shapes are identical?

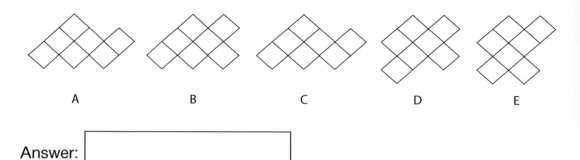

A   B   C   D   E

Answer: [   ]

Q20. Which of the following 2 shapes are identical?

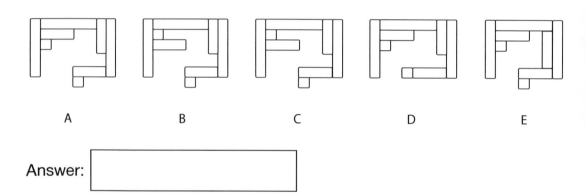

A   B   C   D   E

Answer: [   ]

Once you have completed the exercise please check your answers carefully.

ANSWERS TO SPATIAL REASONING TEST EXERCISE 6

Q1. A + E

Q2. B + C

Q3. D + A

Q4. B + E

Q5. A + E

Q6. B + C

Q7. D + E

Q8. D + B

Q9. A + C

Q10. D + E

Q11. B + D

Q12. B + E

Q13. A + C

Q14. A + E

Q15. B + D

Q16. A + C

Q17. B + D

Q18. C + E

Q19. A + C

Q20. B + C

Once you are satisfied with your answers, move on to the next section of the guide.

SPATIAL REASONING TESTS

SECTION 7

SPATIAL REASONING TESTS SECTION 7

In this next set of questions you have to identify which of the Answer figures is a rotation of the Question figure. You have to rotate the Question figure in your head and identify which of the Answer figures is the correct answer.

Take a look at the following question:

Q. Which of the Answer figures is a rotation of the Question figure?

Question figure

Answer figures

| A | B | C | D | E |

You will notice that shape E is the only option from the 5 which is identical when rotated. With this type of question be careful not to fall into the trap of looking for 'mirror' images of the Question figure. Instead, make sure you mentally rotate the Question figure in your mind until you identify the correct option from the Answer figures. Once you understand what is required, work through the following exercise as quickly and accurately as possible. There are 20 questions and you have 7 minutes to complete the test.

SPATIAL REASONING TEST EXERCISE 7

Q1. Which of the Answer figures is a rotation of the Question figure?

Question figure

Answer figures

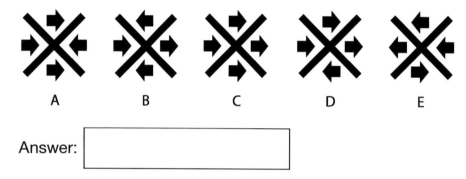

| A | B | C | D | E |

Answer: [   ]

Q2. Which of the Answer figures is a rotation of the Question figure?

Question figure

Answer figures

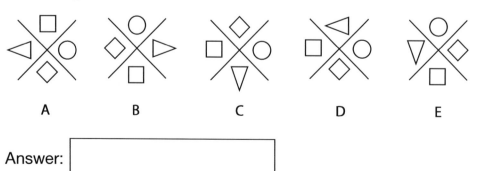

| A | B | C | D | E |

Answer: [   ]

Q3. Which of the Answer figures is a rotation of the Question figure?

Question figure

Answer figures

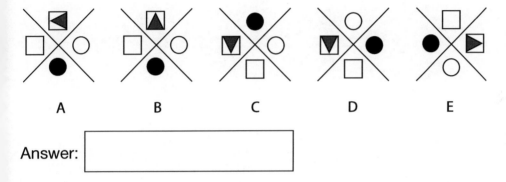

A   B   C   D   E

Answer:

Q4. Which of the Answer figures is a rotation of the Question figure?

Question figure

Answer figures

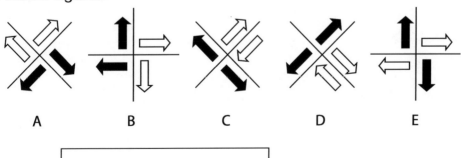

A   B   C   D   E

Answer:

Q5. Which of the Answer figures is a rotation of the Question figure?

Question figure

Answer figures

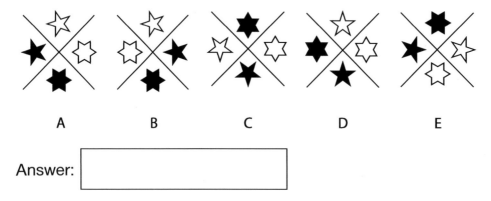

A	B	C	D	E

Answer:

Q6. Which of the Answer figures is a rotation of the Question figure?

Question figure

Answer figures

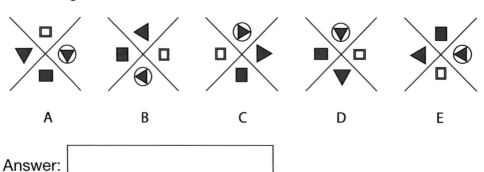

A	B	C	D	E

Answer:

Q7. Which of the Answer figures is a rotation of the Question figure?

Question figure

Answer figures

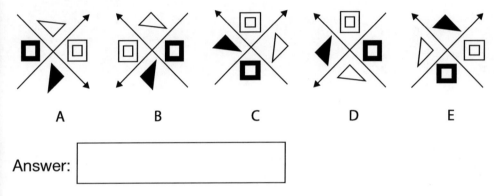

| A | B | C | D | E |

Answer: [   ]

Q8. Which of the Answer figures is a rotation of the Question figure?

Question figure

Answer figures

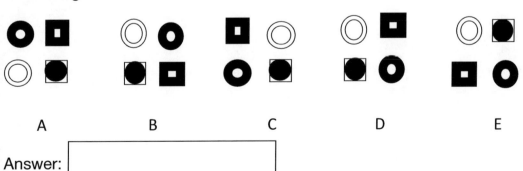

| A | B | C | D | E |

Answer: [   ]

Q9. Which of the Answer figures is a rotation of the Question figure?

Question figure

Answer figures

A   B   C   D   E

Answer:

Q10. Which of the Answer figures is a rotation of the Question figure?

Question figure

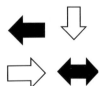

Answer figures

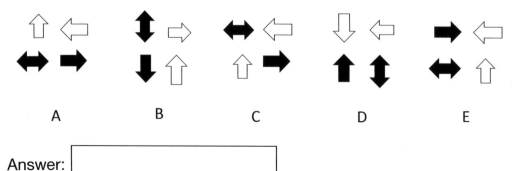

A   B   C   D   E

Answer:

Q11. Which of the Answer figures is a rotation of the Question figure?

Question figure

Answer figures

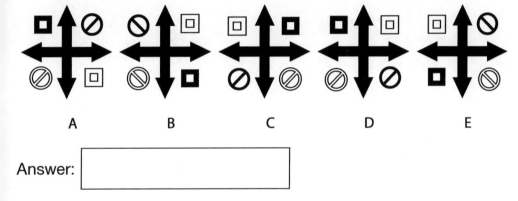

| A | B | C | D | E |

Answer:

Q12. Which of the Answer figures is a rotation of the Question figure?

Question figure

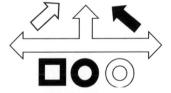

Answer figures

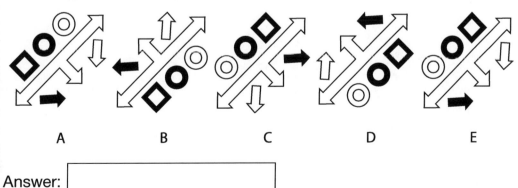

| A | B | C | D | E |

Answer:

Q13. Which of the Answer figures is a rotation of the Question figure?

Question figure

Answer figures

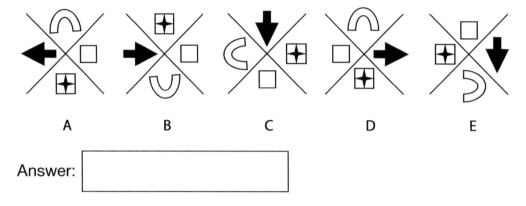

| A | B | C | D | E |

Answer: [   ]

Q14. Which of the Answer figures is a rotation of the Question figure?

Question figure

Answer figures

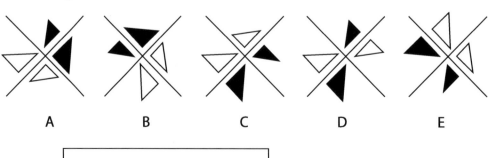

| A | B | C | D | E |

Answer: [   ]

Q15. Which of the Answer figures is a rotation of the Question figure?

Question figure

Answer figures

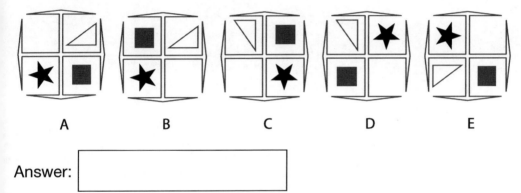

A   B   C   D   E

Answer: [   ]

Q16. Which of the Answer figures is a rotation of the Question figure?

Question figure

Answer figures

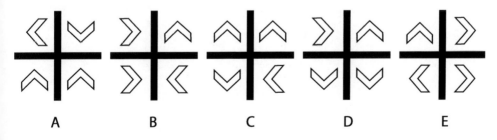

A   B   C   D   E

Answer: [   ]

Q17. Which of the Answer figures is a rotation of the Question figure?

Question figure

Answer figures

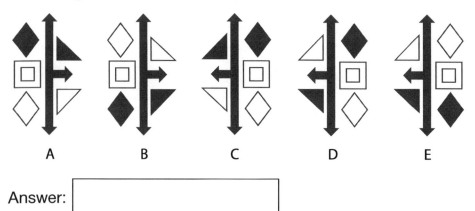

| A | B | C | D | E |

Answer:

Q18. Which of the Answer figures is a rotation of the Question figure?

Question figure

Answer figures

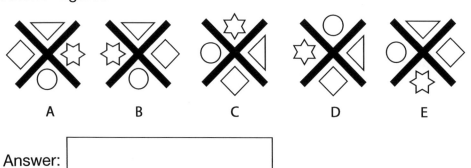

| A | B | C | D | E |

Answer:

Q19. Which of the Answer figures is a rotation of the Question figure?

Question figure

Answer figures

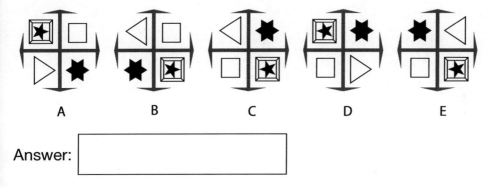

| A | B | C | D | E |

Answer: [   ]

Q20. Which of the Answer figures is a rotation of the Question figure?

Question figure

Answer figures

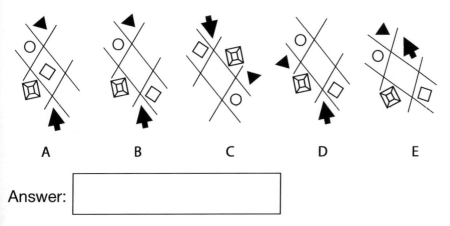

| A | B | C | D | E |

Answer: [   ]

Now check your answers before moving onto the next section of the guide.

ANSWERS TO SPATIAL REASONING TEST EXERCISE 7

Q1. B

Q2. A

Q3. C

Q4. E

Q5. B

Q6. C

Q7. A

Q8. D

Q9. B

Q10. C

Q11. A

Q12. E

Q13. A

Q14. D

Q15. B

Q16. E

Q17. D

Q18. A

Q19. C

Q20. B

Once you are satisfied with your answers, move on to the next section of the guide.

SPATIAL REASONING TESTS

TESTS

SECTION 8

SPATIAL REASONING TESTS SECTION 8

In this next set of questions you have to identify which of the **COMPONENT SHAPES** can be made from the **COMPONENT PARTS**. You decide which of the component shapes is built from the component parts. You need to do this visually and mentally. Shapes CAN be rotated.

Take a look at the following question:

Q. Which of the **COMPONENT SHAPES** can be made from the **COMPONENT PARTS**?

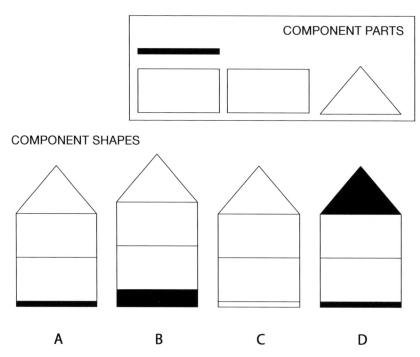

You will notice that **COMPONENT SHAPE A** is the only option from the 4 which can be assembled from the **COMPONENT PARTS**. Once you understand what is required, work through the following exercise as quickly and accurately as possible. There are 20 questions and you have 7 minutes to complete the test.

SPATIAL REASONING TEST EXERCISE 8

Q1. Which of the COMPONENT SHAPES can be made from the COMPONENT PARTS?

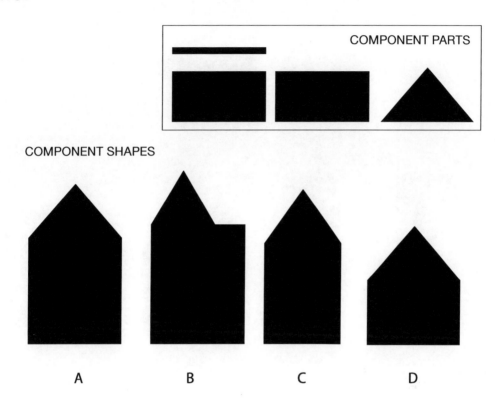

Answer:

Q2. Which of the COMPONENT SHAPES can be made from the COMPONENT PARTS?

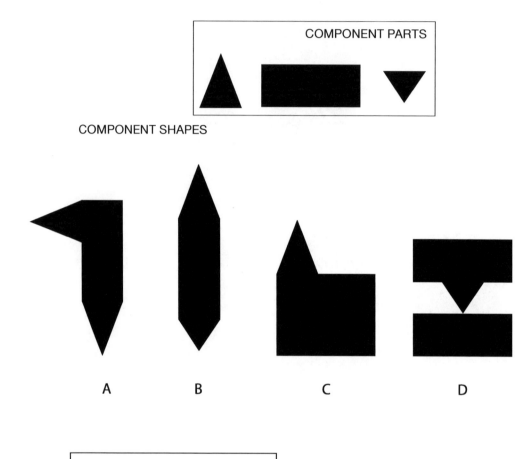

Answer:

Q3. Which of the COMPONENT SHAPES can be made from the COMPONENT PARTS?

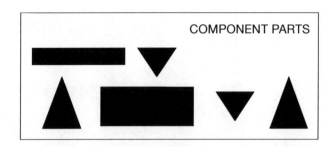

COMPONENT PARTS

COMPONENT SHAPES

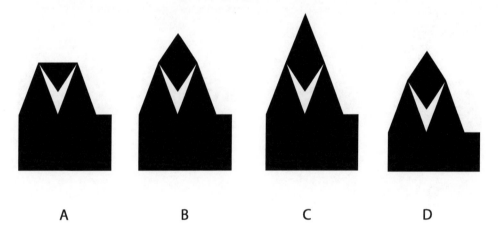

A B C D

Answer:

Q4. Which of the COMPONENT SHAPES can be made from the COMPONENT PARTS?

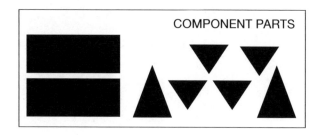

COMPONENT SHAPES

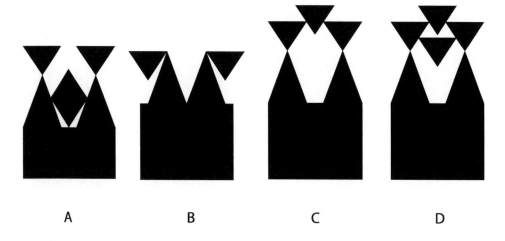

| A | B | C | D |

Answer:

Q5. Which of the COMPONENT SHAPES can be made from the COMPONENT PARTS?

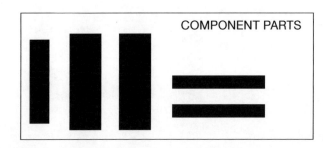

COMPONENT PARTS

COMPONENT SHAPES

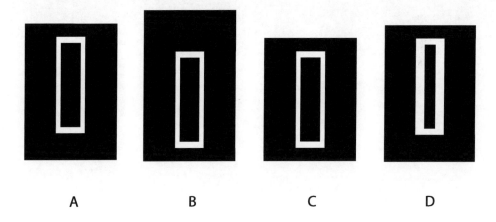

| A | B | C | D |

Answer:

Q6. Which of the COMPONENT SHAPES can be made from the COMPONENT PARTS?

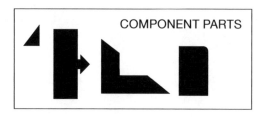

COMPONENT PARTS

COMPONENT SHAPES

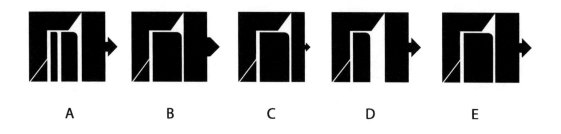

| A | B | C | D | E |

Answer: [ ]

Q7. Which of the COMPONENT SHAPES can be made from the COMPONENT PARTS?

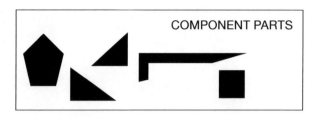

COMPONENT SHAPES

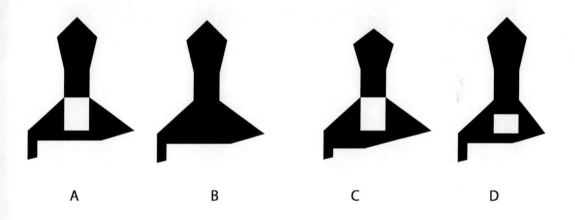

A   B   C   D

Answer:

Q8. Which of the COMPONENT SHAPES can be made from the COMPONENT PARTS?

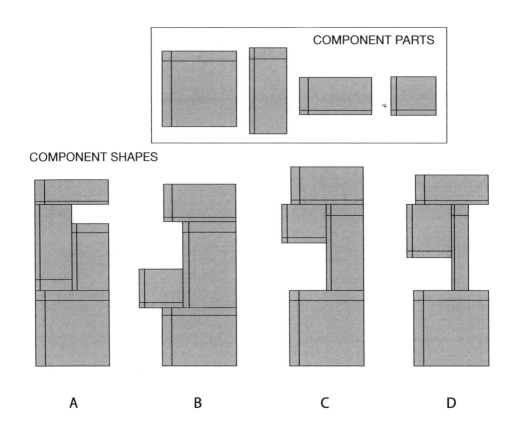

COMPONENT PARTS

COMPONENT SHAPES

A   B   C   D

Answer:

Q9. Which of the COMPONENT SHAPES can be made from the COMPONENT PARTS?

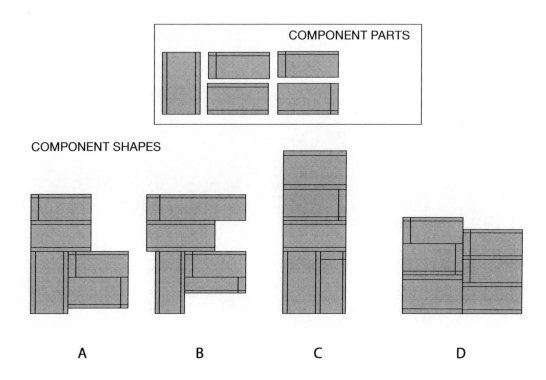

COMPONENT PARTS

COMPONENT SHAPES

A   B   C   D

Answer:

Q10. Which of the COMPONENT SHAPES can be made from the COMPONENT PARTS?

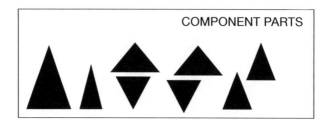

COMPONENT SHAPES

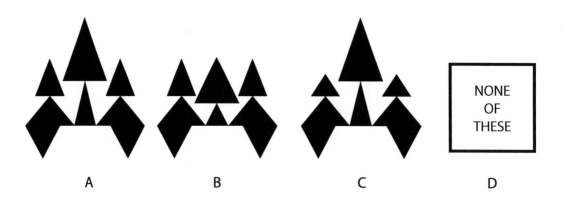

| A | B | C | D |

Answer:

Q11. Which of the COMPONENT SHAPES can be made from the COMPONENT PARTS?

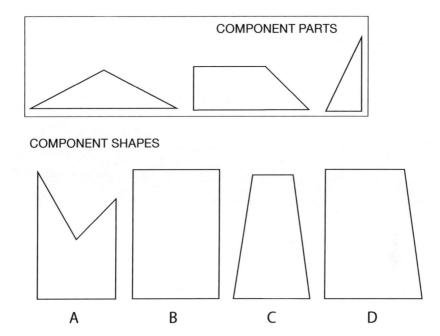

COMPONENT PARTS

COMPONENT SHAPES

A   B   C   D

Answer:

Q12. Which of the COMPONENT SHAPES can be made from the COMPONENT PARTS?

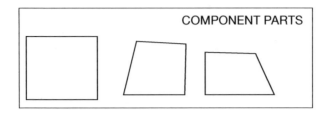

COMPONENT SHAPES

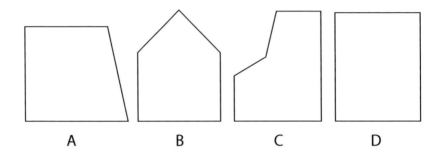

A   B   C   D

Answer:

Q13. Which of the COMPONENT SHAPES can be made from the COMPONENT PARTS?

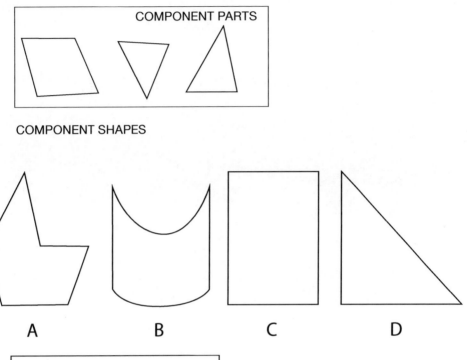

COMPONENT SHAPES

A   B   C   D

Answer:

Q14. Which of the COMPONENT SHAPES can be made from the COMPONENT PARTS?

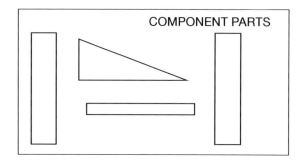

COMPONENT PARTS

COMPONENT SHAPES

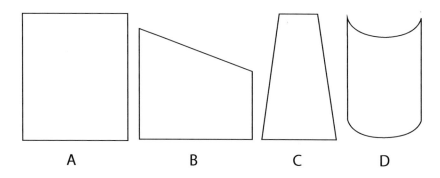

A   B   C   D

Answer:

Q15. Which of the COMPONENT SHAPES can be made from the COMPONENT PARTS?

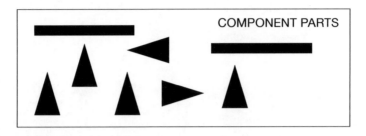

COMPONENT PARTS

COMPONENT SHAPES

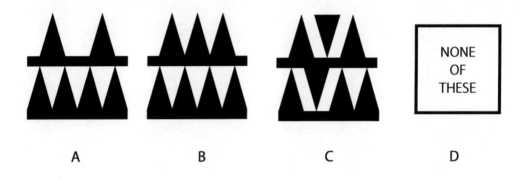

A   B   C   D

Answer: [ ]

Q16. Which of the COMPONENT SHAPES can be made from the COMPONENT PARTS?

COMPONENT PARTS

COMPONENT SHAPES

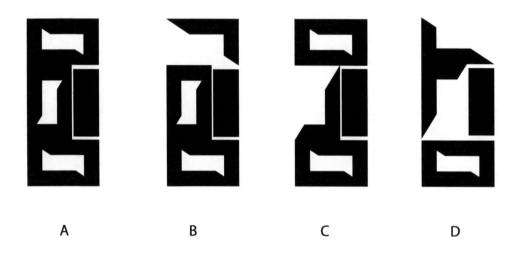

A   B   C   D

Answer:

Q17. Which of the COMPONENT SHAPES can be made from the COMPONENT PARTS?

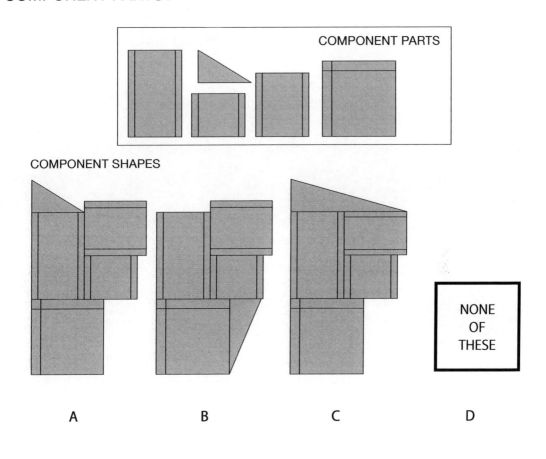

COMPONENT PARTS

COMPONENT SHAPES

A   B   C   D

NONE
OF
THESE

Answer:

Q18. Which of the COMPONENT SHAPES can be made from the COMPONENT PARTS?

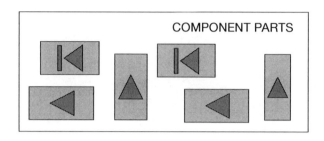

COMPONENT SHAPES

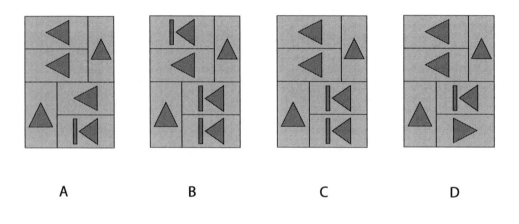

| A | B | C | D |

Answer:

Q19. Which of the COMPONENT SHAPES can be made from the COMPONENT PARTS?

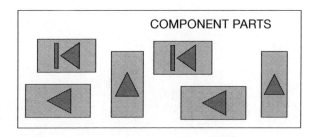

COMPONENT PARTS

COMPONENT SHAPES

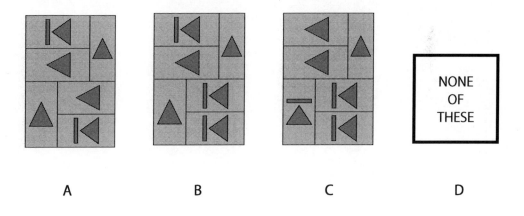

A   B   C   D

Answer:

Q20. Which of the COMPONENT SHAPES can be made from the COMPONENT PARTS?

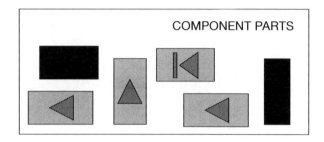

COMPONENT SHAPES

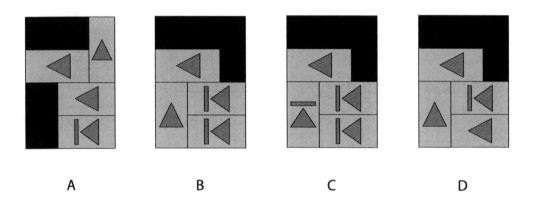

| A | B | C | D |

Answer: [   ]

Once you have completed the test please check your answers.

ANSWERS TO SPATIAL REASONING TEST EXERCISE 8

Q1. A

Q2. B

Q3. B

Q4. D

Q5. C

Q6. E

Q7. A

Q8. C

Q9. A

Q10. A

Q11. A

Q12. C

Q13. A

Q14. B

Q15. A

Q16. A

Q17. A

Q18. C

Q19. A

Q20. D

A FEW FINAL WORDS

You have now reached the end of the testing guide and no doubt you will be ready to take your spatial reasoning test/assessment.

The majority of candidates who pass their test have a number of common attributes. These are as follows:

1. They believe in themselves.

The first factor is self-belief. Regardless of what anyone tells you, you can pass your spatial reasoning test or assessment and secure your chosen job. Just like any selection test, you have to be prepared to work hard in order to be successful. Make sure you have the self-belief to pass the selection process and fill your mind with positive thoughts.

2. They prepare fully.

The second factor is preparation. Those people who achieve in life prepare fully for every eventuality and that is what you must do when you apply for any job or promotion. Work very hard and especially concentrate on your weak areas.

3. They persevere.

Perseverance is a fantastic word. Everybody comes across obstacles or setbacks in their life, but it is what you do about those setbacks that is important. If you fail at something, then ask yourself 'why' you have failed. This will allow you to improve for next time and if you keep improving and trying, success will eventually follow. Apply this same method of thinking when you prepare for the spatial reasoning test.

4. They are self-motivated.

How much do you want this job? Do you want it, or do you really want it?

When you apply for any job you should want it more than anything in the world. Your levels of self-motivation will shine through on your application and during your interview. For the weeks and months leading up to the selection process, be motivated as best you can and always keep your fitness levels up as this will serve to increase your levels of enthusiasm and concentration.

Work hard, stay focused and be what you want…

Richard McMunn

P.S. Don't forget, you can get FREE access to more tests online at:

www.PsychometricTestsOnline.co.uk

Take a look at our other Reasoning guides!

Each guide is packed full of examples and practice questions, to ensure that you make the most out of your revision time and can aim to achieve 100%!

FOR MORE INFORMATION ON OUR TESTING GUIDES, PLEASE CHECK OUT THE FOLLOWING:

WWW.HOW2BECOME.COM

Get Access To
FREE
Reasoning
Test Questions

www.MyPsychometricTests.co.uk

11305010R00123

Printed in Great Britain
by Amazon